THE
LIVERPOOL
MISCELLANY

THE
LIVERPOOL
MISCELLANY

BY LEO MOYNIHAN

VSP

Vision Sports Publishing
19–23 High Street
Kingston upon Thames
Surrey KT1 1LL

www.visionsp.co.uk

Published by Vision Sports Publishing 2008
Reprinted 2009

Text © Leo Moynihan
Illustrations © Bob Bond Sporting Caricatures

ISBN 13: 978-1-905326-46-4

Printed and bound in the UK by MPG Books, Bodmin

Typeset by Palimpsest Book Production Limited,
Grangemouth, Stirlingshire

A CIP catalogue record for this book is
available from the British Library

To the 96 fans who lost their lives at Hillsborough on 15th April 1989.

Foreword
By Ian Rush

Having played just the one season with Juventus, it became clear in the summer of 1988 that I would be leaving. I immediately had Alex Ferguson on the phone asking me to join Manchester United. Uli Hoeness of Bayern Munich was ringing me, my old team-mate Graeme Souness at Rangers, Roma were keen, even Colin Harvey, the manager at Everton was on at me to join him at Goodison Park. I had plenty of options. Then Kenny Dalglish got on the phone and from there it must have been the quickest deal ever made.

"You're on a plane in the morning, you're coming back and you're signing for us." That was that. I was coming home. Thank you very much.

Home is what Liverpool has become for me. That's why it's such a privilege to be involved with a book like this one that really brings out the passion of the club and its fans. The history of this place is so important and this book gives you an insight into what has gone into making the club great and who the people were who made this club what it is today.

I have been fascinated by the facts and figures and whilst I may pop up on the next 150 pages or so now and then, today I am just a fan. I was an ex-player for a bit but then went to the Uefa Cup final against Alves in 2001 and immediately got the bug, the fans' bug. It's different. You get carried away on those trips. Since then I've been to Istanbul and Athens. My two boys are big Liverpool supporters as well so we all go as a family.

I remember, though, when the sheer size of the club filled me with dread. Back in 1980 I read in a Sunday paper that Liverpool were interested in me. I took that with a pinch of salt but then Alan Oakes, my manager at Chester, came to me and said, "Liverpool want you, do you want to go?" What a question. I couldn't help but think about all the great players there and honestly didn't think I'd get a game, so I turned them down.

But Bob Paisley wasn't going to take no for an answer and at the end of the season came back, this time taking Alan, myself and my dad to Melwood. What stands out is the way Bob treated me. Kenny Dalglish and Alan Hansen came in and Bob ignored them and focused just on me. He was so casual about everything, we had lunch and I loved the friendly atmosphere. Alan Oakes said to me, "if you don't like it then you can always come back to Chester". Luckily I never had to.

Not that goals came easy at first. My big break came in 1981 when I was picked for the League Cup Final replay against West Ham. David Johnson had got injured and Bob read the team out. "Up front, Kenny and Rushie." I couldn't believe it. I was a bit confused. I had to ask Kenny if I was really in the team.

It took a while but goals soon followed and I was lucky enough to score more for the club than any other player. I'm so proud of that. When you're playing you just get on with your job. It's when you're finished that you look back and think "wow, I did well there".

It's a cliché but records are there to be broken. I'm a fan now and would love to see a player come through and challenge my goalscoring record but the game has changed and I don't know if a player would ever be here that long. I remember Roger Hunt telling me he was the only Liverpool fan gutted that I came back from Italy because it meant I would get closer to his scoring feats. I saw him recently and he is still so proud of being the club's top league scorer. I don't think his will ever be beaten either.

Enjoy the book and look forward to a great future.

You'll Never Walk Alone

Ian Rush

Acknowledgements

First of all I'd like to thank Jim Drewett at Vision Sports Publishing for asking me to wallow for a few months in all things Liverpool, oh and for paying me to do it.

Thanks to Clive Batty for sifting through the words and not gloating (too much) about Chelsea's some-time hoodoo over the Reds.

Thanks to Justyn Barnes for putting my name forward for the job. Thanks to Jill and Mike Field for their never ending hospitality, Steve Done at the Liverpool Museum, Marc Milmo for the loan of the books, my mum, Clare, for keeping my old programmes under the stairs all these years, and my dad, John, for the memories and the old books, and to everyone at ZOO magazine.

A massive thank you to Larry Hannah and his late wife Margaret. Margaret was the wife of a Red, the mum of Reds, the grandmother of Reds and a friend of Reds. She'll Never Walk Alone. Thanks to James Jessop for cheering me up with beer and kebabs after Athens and thanks as ever to Lawrence Hannah for the laughs and the drinks.

A big thank you to Ian Rush for his Foreword. A top goalscorer and a top man.

Thanks to Bob Bond for the brilliant illustrations.

A special thanks to Catherine and to my new baby daughter Daisy and her beautiful smile. The perfect antidote to a dodgy result or another boardroom cock-up.

Finally, a huge thanks to the players (past and present), officials and fans of Liverpool FC, the greatest team in the world. Justice for the 96.

Leo Moynihan

Author's note: All stats in *The Liverpool Miscellany* are correct up until the start of the 2009/10 season.

— A BLUE BEGINNING —

Bill Shankly once famously said, "This city has two great teams, Liverpool and Liverpool Reserves." But there was a time when the city of Liverpool housed only one of the teams we now know; its name, Everton. Its home ground, Anfield.

In the late 1800s a local brewer, astute businessman and keen sports fan by the name of John Houlding had taken on the administration of a *small* club called Everton and convinced two fellow brewers called John and James Orrell to rent him a patch of land opposite his own home on the Anfield Road. Mr Houlding agreed the £100 annual rent and his team had their home. On September 27th 1884, the first ever game was played at Anfield, Everton beating a side called Earlestown 5–0.

Football was becoming more and more popular and under Mr Houlding's stewardship, Everton were known as one of the finest and most organised clubs around, even publishing the first matchday programme. Professionalism was introduced in 1885 and three years later Everton joined forces with 11 other clubs from the north-west and the Midlands and the Football League was born. Everton's first home game of the inaugural 1888/89 season, and therefore the first League game to be staged at Anfield, was on September 8th 1888 against local club Accrington Stanley.

— KICK OFF —

Sometimes, there's nothing like a good row. In 1891, Everton won their first League Championship but all was not well. The club had been formed by strict Methodists who despised the influence of alcohol on Victorian Liverpool and who therefore mistrusted John Houlding, the brewer who ran the club's affairs from the Sandon Hotel, a pub he owned on the Walton Breck Road.

Here, the team would change into their kit before running over the road to the ground, and while that had an effect on Mr Houdling's ringing cash registers, it did little for Everton's professional reputation. Mr Houlding had also decreed that only his beer would be sold at Anfield and soon there were vociferous objections to his role at the club.

Mr Houdling had spent £5,845 to buy the Anfield site from the Orrell brothers and now proposed that the rent should go up from £100 to £250 a year. The publican proposed that Everton's members should turn their club into a limited company and buy the site from him but they opposed any such move and even refused the £250 rent, instead offering only £180. Mr Houlding had spent large amounts of his own money on the club's expenses and couldn't fathom why there were so many who took offence to him making some money back on his investment. "I cannot understand why a gentleman that has done so much for the club and its members should be given such treatment," he wrote.

That treatment was about to get worse. On March 12th 1892 a meeting was called, opinions were given, arguments were fought but unresolved and at the end a rebellious majority led by George Mahon, the organist at the church where Everton had first been formed, voted to leave Mr Houlding and Anfield forever. Good riddance . . .

— OUT WITH THE OLD, IN WITH THE NEW —

After Everton departed Anfield in 1892 John Houlding was left with a football ground, three of his first team squad and a handful of faithful fans (who may well have been after his ale) and a burning question. What next? The answer to that query would of course one day send shockwaves around the European game, but for now that future was far from clear.

Three days after the disbanding of the club and its movement to a site called Goodison Park, Mr Houlding held another meeting at his home at 73 Anfield Road. There he asked for his small band of supporters to back a plan for a new club, which of course they did. Mr Houlding had made enquiries about keeping the name Everton, but the Football League had decreed that the existing club should keep that. It was a great friend of Mr Houlding, William E. Barclay who had an inspired idea. If Everton were to keep their name, why not come up with something that captured the whole city, not just an area of it and it was there and then, on March 15th 1892 that Liverpool Football Club came to be.

— ALL-TIME PREMIERSHIP TABLE —

Here's the top ten in the all-time Premiership table:

Team	P	W	D	L	Pts
1. Man United	658	422	143	93	1409
2. Arsenal	658	352	180	126	1236
3. Chelsea	658	335	176	147	1181
4. LIVERPOOL	658	331	168	159	1161
5. Aston Villa	658	246	198	213	939
6. Newcastle	616	247	165	204	906
7. Tottenham	658	237	174	247	885
8. Everton	658	228	179	251	863
9. Blackburn	582	230	156	196	846
10. West Ham	540	187	135	218	696

— LIVERPOOL'S FIRST MANAGERS —

Long before Roy Evans and Gerard Houllier were glints in the Anfield board's eyes, Liverpool had joint managers. The duo, John McKenna and William Barclay, were charged with getting the new club off the ground and did so with admirable success.

Barclay, a great ally of the club's founder John Houlding, had been involved with the Everton set-up but after the split had stayed loyal to his friend and actually came up with the idea that the team should appeal to the city as a whole and be named 'Liverpool'. McKenna, an Ulsterman by birth, had moved to the city as a nine-year-old and gone on to become a successful businessman whose obvious nous had appealed to Houlding. The founder had made a loan of £500 to the new club to get things started but slowly disappeared from the scene, as McKenna became the main man at Anfield. Both McKenna and Barclay were named directors and took joint control of team affairs.

It was McKenna who travelled to Scotland and took full advantage of the amateur status of the game north of the border, convincing ten Scots to come south and play for his new team. The Lancashire League was easily won in 1893 and both men clearly had an eye for a good player but, if truth be told, McKenna wielded far more influence over how things were done.

McKenna, officially the secretary of the club, wrote a letter and, without anyone else's knowledge, sent it to the Football League requesting immediate election to their growing party. The first Barclay knew of it (and he was sceptical about a move to the league as he felt it was too soon) was a telegram he received requesting their attendance at a meeting to arrange fixtures for the forthcoming season. Despite that difference of opinion, both men did their very best for the fledgling club, guiding the new players to great heights and winning two Second Division titles.

Soon, however, it became apparent that a fully-fledged football man was needed and McKenna appointed Tom Watson who had made his name at Sunderland. McKenna, however, remained very much part of the Anfield fabric, looking after administration and later enjoying two spells as chairman (1904–14 and 1917–19). A staunch football man, 'Honest John' (a nickname he picked up due to his renowned integrity) was chairman of the Football League from 1910 until his death aged 82, in 1936.

McKenna and Barclay fact-file

Games in charge 181

Honours	Season
Lancashire League	1892/93
Division Two Championship	1893/94
Division Two Championship	1895/96

— COME ON YOU MIGHTY BLUE AND WHITES! —

It may seem sacrilege to some but Liverpool haven't always played in red – in fact, they started out in the blue and white kits left by the departing Everton in 1892.

It is not known exactly when the club converted to their famous red shirts, but the change had certainly been made by the start of the 1896/97 season. Just weeks into that campaign, the *Liverpool Echo* described Liverpool as wearing "red jackets" when they faced West Bromwich Albion at Anfield on October 31st 1896 and a week later, the same paper talked of the roar as Liverpool's "Scarlet Runners" took to the field at Everton for a league game. Come on, you red men!

— CELEBRITY FANS —

Many of the millions of fans who support Liverpool around the world are famous in their own right. Here's a selection of them:

Cilla Black	Singer
Stan Boardman	Comedian
Mel C	Sporty Spice in The Spice Girls
Craig Charles	Actor (*Red Dwarf*)
Darren Clarke	Golfer
Kelly Dalglish	Sky Sports
Laura Davies	Golfer
Chris De Burgh	Singer
Les Dennis	Comedian/TV presenter
Kirsty Gallagher	TV presenter
Mark Owen	Take That singer
Jimmy Tarbuck	Comedian
Dr Dre	Hip-Hop Artist
DJ Spoony	DJ/Radio presenter
Elvis Costello	Musician
Samuel L Jackson	Actor
Mike Myers	Actor (*Austin Powers*)
Michael Howard	Former leader of the Conservative Party
Sue Johnston	Actress (*Brookside, The Royle Family*)
Ricky Tomlinson	Actor (*Brookside, The Royle Family*)
Coleen McLoughlin	Mrs Rooney

— A LONG SHOT —

At the beginning of the 2005/06 season, Liverpool fan Adrian Howard put a £200 bet down at 125–1 that Spanish midfielder Xabi Alonso would, at some time during the course of the season, score from inside his own half. On January 7th 2006 Liverpool were playing Luton in a thrilling FA Cup tie at Kenilworth Road. The Reds had been 3–1 down but came back to lead 4–3.

As the game went into injury time, Alonso received the ball deep in his own half. Luton's keeper had ventured forward for a late corner and so Alonso took a couple of strides before hitting it from 60 yards and watching as the ball sailed into the empty net. Liverpool were through and the lucky punter was £25,000 richer.

— WHY RAFA? —

Before joining Liverpool, Rafa Benitez's Valencia team had twice beaten Liverpool in the Champions League in the 2002/03 season, but there was more to him than just those two victories. Here's his record in Spain with Valencia:

Honours	Season
La Liga	2002, 2004
Uefa Cup	2004

— A SPORTING ALL-ROUNDER —

Liverpool have had plenty of players who during the summer moonlighted at cricket but none excelled quite like South African goalscorer Gordon Hodgson. Signed in 1925, Hodgson was a huge success at Liverpool, lifting the mood and at last giving the thousands of Kopites a hero they could worship like their neighbours did Dixie Dean.

On the cricket field, Hodgson was a brilliant fast bowler and although he never concentrated on the game as he did with football, he managed to play 56 times for Lancashire, scoring 256 runs and taking 148 wickets.

— THEY SAID IT —

"If Lord Snowdon had walked into his office, Shanks probably wouldn't have bothered too much about him, but if some lads from the Kop had walked in, he would have been as nice as pie."
Kevin Keegan on Shankly's love of the people

"I love Liverpool so much that if I caught one of their players in bed with my missus, I'd tiptoe downstairs to make him a cup of tea."
A fan

"In my younger days I was in love with Kevin Keegan and Kenny Dalglish and Graeme Souness. Liverpool was my team."
Jose Mourinho

"At last, we've found the new Jimmy Greaves."
Jimmy Greaves on Michael Owen

"It's a bit like being an orphan and then you join a good family."
Ron Yeats on coming to Liverpool

"Listen I honestly believe that Liverpool were the instigators of Total Football, despite what the Dutch might say."
Phil Thompson

"After the game, I went round the chippy with my mates and got a big kiss from my Mum when I got home."
Robbie Fowler after scoring five goals against Fulham in 1993

"Arsenal? Spurs? No chance! The best two clubs in London are still Stringfellow's and the Hippodrome."
Terry McDermott

"He is to Liverpool what De Gaulle is to France."
Gerard Houlllier on Bill Shankly

"A man who even sees red in his dreams and flies in imagination with the Liver-bird."
Geoffery Green, *The Times*, on Bill Shankly

"I wasn't particularly special as a player, but when Rushie kept scoring from my crosses I was made to look good."
Craig Johnston

"I haven't forgotten my roots or whatever. I see myself and the fans on the same level. I don't see myself on a pedestal."
Jamie Carragher

Interviewer: "Ever done anything flash to earn a ribbing from the boys back in Bootle?"
Jamie Carragher: "I remember I got a wallet once and got slaughtered for that.
Interviewer: "You mean a fancy Gucci number, with special Premiership-footballer, super-expensive leather?"
Jamie Carragher: "Nah, just a normal wallet. Where I'm from, you carry money in your pockets, and I got slaughtered by my mates. I'd never had a wallet before and they thought I was trying to be someone I'm not. I got rid of it. Never had one since."

"The Kop is not the members' enclosure at Ascot, and nor does it regret it."
Arthur Hopcraft, writer

Joe Fagan: "What would you like to drink?"
Elton John: "A Pink Gin please."
Joe Fagan: "Sorry lad, you can have a brown ale, a Guinness or a Scotch like the rest of us."

"Tommy Smith wasn't born – he was quarried."
Football commentator David Coleman on Tommy Smith

"I always thought Anfield was a place more beautiful than heaven."
John Aldridge

— QUIDS IN AND QUIDS OUT —

Liverpool's most expensive signing is Fernando Torres. The Spanish striker signed from Atletico Madrid in July 2007 cost the club £21m. The most money the club has ever received for a player was in 2001 when Leeds coughed up £12.75m for Robbie Fowler.

— GREAT GAFFERS: BILL SHANKLY OBE (1959–1974) —

The legendary Bill Shankly

Football men come and they go. The moments they create linger in the memory but are somehow always destined to be replaced by those that follow them. Not all football men, however, are Bill Shankly. Despite Liverpool Football Club achieving so much, giving their legion of fans so many incredible moments to savour since he retired in 1974, it is him and his image that still prevails, watching over the club like a proud great-grandfather. Even today's young fans wear T-shirts adorned with his image, they sing songs about him, and they lap up stories about his legendry quips. Whatever happens in the future, whatever changes the new owners' dollars bring, the name of Bill Shankly is ingrained in the club and it always will be.

American millionaires would have choked on their hot dogs back in December 1959 at the very suggestion of investing in Liverpool FC. The team was as run down as the stadium in which it played but Shankly saw something in the place that made him believe the Reds could be the best. That glimmer of hope was the supporters who came in their thousands to support the team, despite the constant disappointment of missing out on promotion. It was those long-suffering fans Shankly wanted to reward.

After an illustrious playing career at Preston North End, Shankly managed Carlisle, Grimsby, Workington and Huddersfield but he felt those were just seats of learning for his life's work and he arrived at Liverpool determined to make them the best around, "a bastion of invincibility". He took stock, got rid of 24 of his playing staff, organised the men behind the scenes and slowly his Liverpool began to take shape. Ron Yeats and Ian St John arrived; Roger Hunt, the young forward inherited by Shankly, began to flourish under his tutelage; and in 1962, the club demolished their Second Division rivals and returned to the top flight.

Success didn't end there. The championship was won in 1964, the FA Cup was finally claimed the following year, followed by another title. Beatlemania may have been gripping the world but for those Kopites who lived for their Saturday, the Fab Four were just providing a soundtrack to what really mattered.

Shankly's team was like him: dedicated, quick-witted and entertaining. He was a master motivator who got the best out of his players and made them believe that they could take on the world. Kevin Keegan – part of the second great team that Shankly built – recalls how his manager once watched the legendary Bobby Moore get off the team bus as it arrived at Anfield. "He said to me, 'Don't worry about him – he's been in the nightclubs again. He's limping, he's got bags under his eyes, and he's got dandruff.'"

Liverpool went on to win another championship in 1973, the Uefa Cup (the club's first European trophy) in the same year and the FA Cup in 1974. That Wembley victory, though, was to be his last game in charge. Shankly had put everything into making Liverpool the best team in England and wanted to spend more time with his wife and grown-up kids. His resignation came as a massive blow; fans were stunned, refusing to believe national news crews sent to the city to gauge reaction.

Shankly, who died in September 1981, was adored by the fans and he, in turn, always acknowledged their central role in Liverpool's accumulation of silverware. "Success brought happiness to the supporters," he later wrote. "That was *the* great thing."

Bill Shankly fact-file

Games in charge	783

Honours	Season
Second Division Championship	1961/62
First Division Championship	1963/64
Charity Shield	1964*
FA Cup	1965
Charity Shield	1965*
First Division Championship	1965/66
Charity Shield	1966
First Division Championship	1972/73
Uefa Cup	1972/73
FA Cup	1974

* Shared trophy

— WATSON STANDS HIS GROUND —

With the outbreak of war in 1914, many football clubs were criticised for continuing to play matches while players who decided against joining the armed forces were given short shrift. Liverpool manager Tom Watson felt the hostile public reaction was unfair and he wrote to *The Times* to air his thoughts and prove the club was doing its bit:

"We have 27 professionals, 13 married and 14 single. Recruiting has taken place at the ground all season, with military bands at all games. One director, one player, a great many shareholders and two sons of directors have joined the army. The players are donating 12 per cent of their salaries to the assistance of the needy and to war funds. The donations have been:

The club:	*£413 7s 6d*
Ground collections:	*£114 3s 5d*
From staff, directors and players:	*£25 15s 9d*

Eighteen footballs have also been sent to the front for supporters in the King's uniform. £10 10s has been sent to Queen Mary's fund. Players are drilled twice a week by a retired army officer. 1,000 soldiers and sailors are given free admission to each match, as are the wounded men and Belgian refugees."

— LIVERPOOL'S BARGAIN XI —

Bill Shankly once described the signing of Kevin Keegan from Scunthorpe for £35,000 as "robbery with violence". It wasn't the first or the last time that Liverpool have bagged themselves a bargain so here is a team of steals:

Ray Clemence
Fee £18,000
Appearances: 664
Goals: 0

Phil Neal	**Alan Hansen**	**Sami Hyypia**	**Steve Nicol**
£66,000	£100,000	£2.5m	£300,000
Apps: 650	Apps: 620	Apps: 464*	Apps: 468
Goals: 59	Goals: 14	Goals: 35*	Goals: 46

Ronnie Whelan	**Graeme Souness**	**John Barnes**
£35,000	£352,000	£900,000
Apps: 493	Apps: 359	Apps: 407
Goals: 73	Goals: 55	Goals: 108

Kevin Keegan	**Kenny Dalglish**
£35,000	£440,000
Apps: 323	Apps: 515
Goals: 100	Goals: 172

Ian Rush
£330,000
Apps: 660
Goals: 346

* Up to and including the 2008/09 season

Total cost: £5,076,000

— JAVIER WANTS A PIZZA THE ACTION —

Javier Mascherano's brother owns a pizza parlour back in San Lorenzo, Argentina and when he goes home you can find Javier kneading the dough and putting on the toppings.

— VIVA EL LIVERPOOL! —

When Liverpool's number 9 Fernando Torres lifted the ball over the hapless Jens Lehmnn in Vienna on June 29th 2008 to score the only goal of the UEFA European Championship Final, Koppites everywhere were cheering over their tapas! The goalscoring hero immediately dedicated his triumph to his new club.

"I would like to thank the staff and players at Liverpool for their support during Euro 2008 because it makes a real difference when you know you have the backing of the people of your club and because of this they share in our success.

"I have had a wonderful first season at Anfield and the goals I scored for Liverpool gave me the confidence and belief I needed for the Euros and, again, I would like to thank Rafa and his staff because I have improved as a player thanks to them.

"But it isn't just the people at the club who have helped me, it is also the supporters and the people of the city. From the moment I first came to Liverpool I have been made to feel welcome and that is why I am able to enjoy my football so much.

"It is incredible because the Liverpool fans have given me so much support and I know that they have even been supporting Spain and this is something I will never forget and I thank everyone for that."

Spain actually included four Liverpool men in their winning squad. Pepe Reina, Alvaro Arbeloa, Xabi Alonso and Fernando Torres. No other club, not even Real Madrid or Barcelona, was as well represented. *Nunca Andarás Sólo* – That's Spanish for "You'll Never Walk Alone".

— KOP THAT —

The last player to score in front of the terraced Kop? Officially, it was Norwich midfielder Jeremy Goss. The Canaries were the visitors for the last home game of the 1993/94 season and it was Goss who scored the only goal of the match in the first half. Unofficially it was mischievous fan, John Garner. With the Kop due to be pulled down and redeveloped that summer, supporters refused to leave in homage to the famous terrace. The players had said their goodbyes and left a ball with some kids at the front. Garner went over and 'borrowed' the ball, clambered onto the pitch, took the applause of the crowd before smashing it into the top right-hand corner of the net. "Was it the best moment of my life?" wonders Garner. "Well put it this way, having kids doesn't even beat hitting the back of the net at the Kop end."

— A NIGHT LIKE NO OTHER —

On March 16th 1977, those present at Anfield saw a match that they would talk about for decades to come.

Liverpool were 1–0 down from their European Cup quarter-final first leg in St Etienne, but the fans were in bullish mood and packed into the ground hours prior to kick-off to ensure a good view. Many, though, were still getting comfortable when Kevin Keegan swung in a second-minute cross that eluded Curkovic in the French goal and nestled in the top corner. Bedlam ensued as the Kop began to chime but the French champions, in their luminous green shirts, were no mugs. They had reached the previous season's final before losing to Bayern Munich and were many people's favourites to go one step further this time.

Five minutes into the second half that particular prophecy looked spot on when Dominque Bathenay, the scorer of St Etienne's goal in the first leg, lashed the ball past Ray Clemence from 25 yards. It was a hammer blow and meant that Liverpool now needed to find two goals. A hush descended on the home terraces while the visiting fans celebrated wildly.

Liverpool, however, regained the lead nine minutes later when a typically intelligent run from Ray Kennedy saw him latch onto a John Toshack flick and the midfielder stroked the ball in at the Kop end. Game on.

With time running out, Liverpool's approach became more gung-ho, throwing everything at the French. One of those weapons was David 'Super sub' Fairclough. With 15 minutes left, Liverpool boss Bob Paisley put his red-haired sub on, telling him to "roam around and pick up some pieces." Just six minutes were left on the clock when Fairclough finally got hold of one of those pieces, courtesy of a lobbed Kennedy pass, and ran with the ball towards goal.

One step, two steps closer to goal, the keeper came out to narrow the angle. Would Fairclough's nerve hold? The man they called the 'bionic carrot' takes up the story: "My first thought was to get the ball out under my feet to make a shooting chance. Once I managed that my next problem was to get the ball past Curkovic, the goalkeeper. My most vivid memory was to at least make sure I hit the target."

Which of course he did, slotting it under the keeper and into the net. "I've been lucky enough to have seen the goal many times since and it doesn't lose any of its drama, I can tell you. It still makes me feel cold, what with the noise and the images of the fans celebrating."

Celebrating isn't the right word; Anfield went insane with pleasure. The team had to defend (and people forget that the French had a couple of late chances to spoil the party) but the fans weren't to be denied. Their team was through to the semi-finals of the European Cup on a night they would never forget.

— THE BIRTH OF A LEGEND —

It's been called Liverpool's twelfth man. It's been credited for giving Liverpool a goal advantage even before a ball has been kicked in anger. Wherever in the world there are football fans and wherever they stand or sit in worship of their football team, those supporters will have heard of Liverpool's Spion Kop.

Once a mass sprawl of terracing, it now seats 12,409 fans but it started life in 1906 as a gift from the club to its growing number of eager fans. Liverpool had just won their second league title in front of an average home crowd of 18,000 and so the board authorized that the southern end of the ground, on Walton Breck Road should be expanded.

And so an immense, roofless mound of soil and cinders was built behind the goal offering fans a fine view in time for the start of the 1906/07 season. But what would it be called?

The Boer War was still fresh in the minds of many Liverpool families, especially one of it's most bloody battles in 1900 on a South African hill called Spioenkop. There, 300 men from the Lancashire Fusiliers had lost their lives, many of them recruited from the Merseyside area. Ernest Jones, the editor of the *Liverpool Daily Post and Echo*, suggested the new terrace be named after the battle.

Despite the north-western connection, the name was already being used in south London at Manor Field, the home of Woolwich Arsenal who had adopted the name 'Kop' for a raised area of terracing in 1904. However, it was Liverpool's 'Kop' that would stick, stand the test of time and eventually become the envy of the football world.

When the new viewing area was unveiled, the press were hugely impressed. The *Athletic News* wrote: "Liverpool, having provided themselves with a up-to-date enclosure, now possess a home worthy of their title as league champions . . . when completed the ground will be the equal to anything in the country."

— A QUESTION OF SPORT —

Since the show first aired in 1970, three Liverpool men have captained sides on *A Question of Sport*. They are:

Emlyn Hughes
Michael Owen
Neil Ruddock

— WALK ON, WALK ON . . . —

When you walk through a storm, hold your head up high
And don't be afraid of the dark.
At the end of the storm there's a golden sky
And the sweet, silver song of a lark.
Walk on through the wind, walk on through the rain,
Though your dreams be tossed and blown.
Walk on, walk on with hope in your heart,
And you'll never walk alone.
You'll never walk alone.

The flags are waving, a sea of scarves are held proudly aloft and vocal chords are stretched to their absolute limit. It must be Anfield. It must be 'You'll Never Walk Alone'. Is there a better sight in English football than a packed Anfield, led by a heaving Kop before a big match, singing its world famous anthem?

The song itself, however, started as a show-tune. Written by legendary impresarios Richard Rogers and Oscar Hammerstein II, for their 1945 musical *Carousel*, 'YNWA' is first sung to comfort the character of Julie Jordon after the death of her husband Billy Bigelow. The song is later reprised at the graduation of their daughter and is once more used as the show's final crescendo.

'YNWA' was an immediate hit with the public; hitting the right note with the many families who had lost loved ones in the Second World War. In 1945, Frank Sinatra (his eyes might have been blue but his song was red) got to number nine in the American charts and has been followed there by the likes of Nina Simone (1959), Patti LaBelle (1964) and Elvis Presley (1968).

In this country, the song was a hit for Merseybeat band Gerry and the Pacemakers who stayed at number one for four weeks from October 26th 1963 and was quickly adopted by the all singing and all swaying Kop end. It is said that the Kop would sing along to whatever the number one was on the day and as 'YNWA' was there for four straight weeks it stuck. Since then 'YNWA' has become synonymous with the club but has continued to be used all over the world.

— RUSH'S FA CUP FINAL MAGIC —

Ian Rush has scored more FA Cup final goals than any other player in history. His first final in 1986 saw him score two against Everton, three years later he did the same against the same opponents before grabbing a fifth in the 2–0 win over Sunderland in 1992.

— PLAYERS WHO SHOOK THE KOP —

In 2006, more than 110,000 Liverpool fans voted for the players they felt had had the biggest effect on Liverpool Football Club.

Here is the top ten:

Player	Seasons
1. Kenny Dalglish	1977–90
2. Steven Gerrard	1998–
3. Ian Rush	1980–1987 and 1988–1996
4. Robbie Fowler	1993–2001 and 2006–2007
5. John Barnes	1987–1997
6. Billy Liddell	1946–1960
7. Jamie Carragher	1997–
8. Kevin Keegan	1971–1977
9. Graeme Souness	1978–1984
10. Emlyn Hughes	1967–1979

— MORE 'YNWA' FACTS —

- Pink Floyd used a recording of the Kop singing 'You'll Never Walk Alone' on the track 'Fearless' on their 1971 album *Meddle*. The fans' repeated chant of 'Liverpool!' is also used at the conclusion of the song.
- Following the 1985 Bradford disaster, 'YNWA' was recorded by a group of artists called The Crowd which included Gerry Marsden (of Gerry and the Pacemakers), Paul McCartney and Rolf Harris. It got to number one in the UK charts for two weeks.
- In 1998 'YNWA' was performed by the Three Tenors, Luciano Pavarotti, Placido Domingo and Jose Carreras and reached number 21 in the UK charts.
- The song can also be heard on the BBC radio play of *The Hitchhikers Guide to the Galaxy*, an episode of the US sitcom *Cheers* and it appears on a recent Led Zeppelin DVD with the crowd singing it at the end of their 1979 Knebworth performance. A version is also played during the end credits of Peter Jackson's 1994 film *Heavenly Creatures*.

— RED LEGENDS: GRAEME SOUNESS —

For the second leg of their European Cup semi-final in 1984, Liverpool travelled to Romania with a slim 1–0 lead that the fans of Dinamo Bucharest felt they could easily turn over.

It was going to be an intimidating affair, the hostile atmosphere only intensified by an incident at Anfield that left one of the Romanian players with a broken jaw. Dinamo were blaming one man, Graeme Souness. It was he who was supposed to have caught the Romanian with an off-the-ball punch, and now in their home stadium they meant to make him pay.

Lesser men and lesser players would have hidden from the confrontation; they would have gone missing, but not Souness. As the team strolled onto the pitch with the whistles cascading down upon them, Souness visibly grew in stature and went on to play one of his best ever games for the club. Drawing power from the fans' angry reception, he led the team to a 2–1 win, on to Rome and ultimately to a fourth European Cup victory.

That European triumph was to be Souness' last for the club, and it says a lot about the man that the season following his departure for Sampdoria was the club's first without a trophy in nine years.

Souness arrived from Middlesbrough midway through the 1977/78 season and went straight into the team for a win at West Bromwich Albion. A month into his Liverpool career, Manchester United came to Anfield and any fans who weren't yet sure about their new signing were convinced when he ran onto a cross and from the edge of the box cracked a volley into the top corner at the Anfield Road end.

His hero status was further ensured that season when he laid on the pass for Kenny Dalglish to win the European Cup against Bruges. The following season he became the hub of possibly the greatest midfield the club, or the country has ever seen. McDermott, Ray Kennedy, Case and Souness proved a formidable quartet. Once described as, "a bear of a player with the delicacy of a violinist", Souness was the perfect midfielder, a master at breaking up opposition attacks but equally potent at making and scoring goals. His hat-trick against CSKA Sofia at Anfield on route to European Cup glory in 1981 will long live in the memory.

In 1984, Souness decided he needed a new challenge, heading off to Italy where once more he would be loved by the fans. He would, of course, return to Anfield as manager but it is as a player that Liverpool fans will always remember him.

Graeme Souness fact-file

Appearances	358
Goals	56
Scotland caps while at Liverpool	37

Honours	Seasons
First Division Championship	1978/79
	1979/80
	1981/82
	1982/83
	1983/84
League Cup	1980/81
	1981/82
	1982/83
	1983/84
European Cup	1980/81
	1983/84
Charity Shield	1979
	1980
	1982

— LIVERPOOL'S YOUNGEST EVER GOALSCORER —

Fifty-seven minutes into the penultimate game of Liverpool's 1996/97 season, Liverpool were plodding along against Wimbledon at Selhurst Park. The title race was all but lost as the Dons took a 2–0 lead. Stan Collymore had drifted out of the game and it was his number that came up to be substituted as manager Roy Evans decided now was the time to use what he soon hoped would be his not so secret weapon.

Michael Owen had scored goals galore at all levels of the game and took to the field as a 17-year-old clearly unimpressed with reputations such as that of Vinnie Jones in the Wimbledon midfield. Just 17 minutes after coming on, the blisteringly fast striker dashed onto a through ball and strode purposefully towards the Wimbledon goal. He had plenty of time to think about the situation, plenty of time to be put off by the enormity of the situation, but instead he simply did what he'd done since early childhood; he moved the ball onto his right foot and slipped it under the goalkeeper into the goal, and in doing so he became the youngest player to ever score a goal for Liverpool FC.

— RED ALL OVER —

For years Liverpool had worn red shirts with white shorts and socks. In the early 1960s under Bill Shankly success was becoming commonplace but the astute boss wanted more. He believed that his team would look more menacing with red shorts and asked his 6ft 2ins 'colossus' Ron Yeats to model for him.

"Bloody hell, you look eight feet tall," exclaimed Ian St John who was there at the time and suggested his boss go one step further and try red socks as well.

On November 25th 1964, Liverpool ran out at Anfield to play Anderlecht in the European Cup, wearing their new imposing colours for the first time. The Belgians were beaten 3–0 and Yeats got the third. One of only 16 he scored in 454 appearances.

— CHEERS, EL TEL —

Terry Venables may be about as Scouse as jellied eels, but the chirpy cockney did help the Reds in their quest for a first FA Cup back in 1965.

Liverpool had played a European Cup quarter-final replay on the Thursday night and travelled back from Rotterdam, knowing they had less than 48 hours to recover and take on Chelsea in the semi-final of the FA Cup at Villa Park.

Chelsea were no mugs. Their manager Tommy Docherty had assembled a fine young team boasting the likes of Peter Bonetti, George Graham and, of course, Venables himself. The latter was so confident of overcoming a supposedly tired Liverpool that he had called on some printer mates to make up an FA Cup final souvenir brochure to celebrate Chelsea's inevitable appearance in the showpiece event.

However, somehow Shankly got hold of the magazine and took great delight in sharing Venables' handiwork with his squad just hours before the match.

"We were knackered," recalled Tommy Smith. "We were sitting in the dressing-room before the game when Shankly came in fuming and pinned this brochure to the wall. 'You won't believe it,' he told us, 'but those cocky lot think they're in the final already. Look! They've made up a mock brochure for the final.' Shanks was fuming and so were we."

The effect was a resounding 2–0 win for Liverpool.

— WORLD CUP REDS —

"We're by far the greatest team, the world has ever seen." To Kopites everywhere that may be so, but there is a small competition called the World Cup that shouldn't be forgotten and over the years a number of Liverpool players have contributed to the tournament's matches:

World Cup	Player	Country
1950	Laurie Hughes	England
1958	Alan A'Court	England
	Tommy Younger	Scotland
1966	Roger Hunt	England
	Ian Callaghan	England
1978	Kenny Dalglish	Scotland
	Graeme Souness	Scotland
1982	Phil Neal	England
	Phil Thompson	England
	Kenny Dalglish	Scotland
	Graeme Souness	Scotland
	Alan Hansen	Scotland
1986	Steve Nicol	Scotland
	Jan Molby	Denmark
1990	John Barnes	England
	Peter Beardsley	England
	Steve McMahon	England
	Gary Gillespie	Scotland
	Steve Staunton	Republic of Ireland
	Ray Houghton	Republic of Ireland
	Ronnie Whelan	Republic of Ireland
	Glenn Hysen	Sweden
1994	Ronnie Whelan	Republic of Ireland
	Stig Inge Bjornebye	Norway
1998	Michael Owen	England
	Paul Ince	England
	Steve McManaman	England
	Stig Inge Byornebye	Norway
	Oyvind Leonharsden	Norway
	Brad Freidel	USA

2002	Michael Owen	England
	Emile Heskey	England
	El Hadji Diouf	Senegal
	Jerzey Dudek	Poland
	Dietmar Hamann	Germany
2006	Steven Gerrard	England
	Peter Crouch	England
	Jamie Carragher	England
	Xabi Alonso	Spain
	Luis Garcia	Spain
	Harry Kewell	Australia

— IN THE RED CORNER! —

In 1944, the heavyweight champion of the world signed for Liverpool. Before the war, Joe Louis had claimed the title from James J. Braddock and taken revenge on Germany's Max Schmeling (he lost their first fight in 1936), before joining the army and coming to Europe to fight the Nazis.

It was as a soldier that the champ came to town on a promotional tour and was convinced to sign on the dotted line by Liverpool's then manager, George Kay. Ok, so he never got to do to Everton or Manchester United what he did to countless weary boxers, but officially he was a Liverpool player.

Spookily, Joe Louis defended his title more than any other heavyweight in history. So that's another thing he and Liverpool FC have in common then.

— OUR URUGUAYAN COUSINS —

If ever you should find yourself in downtown Montevideo, Uruguay; hopelessly needing your football fix, then fear not. Help is at hand in the shape of Liverpool Futbol Club who play in their country's Primera Division. Formed in 1915, it is said that the founder members, having attended a geography lesson on the ports of Great Britain agreed that 'Liverpool' would make a great name for a football club. Known as the big underachievers of the Uruguayan game, Liverpool have never won a major trophy. It must be the blue kit they wear!

— A LITTLE HELP FROM YOUR FRIENDS —

Sometimes even the best could do with some help and over the years Liverpool have enjoyed their fair share of charity from the opposition. Liverpool fans of all ages will still take pleasure at seeing a replay of Everton's Sandy Brown hurtling through the air in 1969 and heading past his own keeper to put Liverpool two up. To all of the opposing players who have ever scored an OG for the Reds, we salute you. Here are just a few own goal memories:

- The first own goal to ever go Liverpool's way came in their very first season, on October 20th 1892 in an FA Cup qualifying round against Newtown. Liverpool were 8–0 up when a player called Alfred Townsend popped up to make it nine.
- The very first own goal in league football came on October 17th 1896 at Sunderland when Donald Gow very generously put one through his own goal. Unfortunately, his charity wasn't enough as Liverpool went on to lose 4–3.
- The first league own goal to go Liverpool's way at Anfield came on September 20th 1902 courtesy of Stoke's Leigh Roose who helped Liverpool to a 1–1 draw.
- The first game of the 1959/60 season saw Cardiff City's Danny Malloy score twice for the Reds, the only player to be so kind in one match. Liverpool, however, still managed to lose 3–2. Malloy must have had a soft spot for the Reds, he had also managed to get one in a previous fixture in 1957.
- The most prolific season for own goals came in the championship-winning campaign of 1979/80 when six went Liverpool's way.
- The most vital own goal has to be Liverpool's winner in the 2001 Uefa Cup final against Alaves in Dortmund. With the score level at 4–4 after 90 minutes, it was Delfi Geli who nodded the ball into his own goal to win the Reds their first European trophy in 17 years.

— COUNT THE GOALS —

Liverpool's record wins:

At Anfield: 11–0 v Stromsgodset Drammen, September 17th 1974, European Cup Winners Cup
Away from Anfield: 8–0 v Stoke City, November 29th 2000, League Cup fourth round

— EL NINO'S HALF CENTURY —

On May 24th 2009, Fernando Torres leapt above the Tottenham defence and headed a Dirl Kuyt cross in off the crossbar to notch his 50th goal for Liverpool in only his 84th match.

Torres had reached his milestone quicker than a host of modern greats, including Ian Rush, Kenny Dalglish, Robbie Fowler, Michael Owen and John Aldridge. In fact only Gordon Hodgson, who smashed his first 50 in just 64 games for the Reds in the late 1920's, and Roger Hunt (it took Sir Roger 79 games – albeit a load of those were in the old Second Division), did it quicker.

No wonder the Kop love to bounce in his name. To celebrate here's their song for the striker known as *"The Kid"*.

To the tune of 'The Animals Went in Two by Two . . .'

His Armband proved he was a red, Torres, Torres
'You'll never Walk Alone' it said, Torres, Torres
We bought the lad from sunny Spain,
He gets the ball, he scores again,
Fer-nan-do Torres, Liverpool's Number 9!

La, la, la, la, la, la, la, la, la, la, la, la, la
La, la, la, la, la, la, la, la, la, la, la, la, la
La, la, la, la, la, la, la, la, la, la, la, la, la
Fer-nan-do Torres, Liverpool's Number 9!

[Repeat and Bounce!]

— BAD DAY AT THE OFFICE —

Liverpool's record defeats:

> **At Anfield:** 0–6 v Sunderland, April 19th 1930, First Division
> **Away from Anfield:** 1–9 v Birmingham City, December 11th 1954, Second Division

— RED LEGENDS: KEVIN KEEGAN —

The magnificent 7!

Kevin Keegan's last contribution to the Liverpool cause was probably his most potent. Aware that he was playing his final game for the club, Keegan ran Borussia Monchengladbach's captain Bertie Vogts ragged in the 1977 European Cup final, winning the team their decisive penalty and bidding farewell to the fans with a European Cup winner's medal. Even those supporters who were sceptical of his motives for moving to Hamburg couldn't help but raise a glass that night in Rome to their famous number 7.

Bill Shankly bought Keegan – the player he would later describe as the one who ignited his team of the 1970s – during the build-up to the 1971 FA Cup final against Arsenal. With Wembley on everyone's mind, the £35,000 signing of a 20-year-old from Scunthorpe United was hardly going to grab headlines, but in time Keegan would become the English game's biggest superstar since George Best.

Originally a midfield player (he was actually bought as a replacement for Ian Callaghan), the manager noticed something in Keegan during a pre-season tour in 1971 and gave his new signing a debut at Anfield for the first match of the season as a striker with John Toshack. It took Keegan just 12 minutes to score at the Kop end and his Liverpool career was up and running. Talking of running, Keegan wouldn't stop, and his dedication and workrate made him a hero amongst fans who loved nothing more than a player who gave his all.

Keegan's partnership with Toshack flourished, becoming almost mythical in its potency, with pundits wondering at the pair's telepathy. The two led the line brilliantly for many seasons and despite the resignation of Shankly (a man Keegan considered a second father) their goals continued to win football matches and trophies.

A low point came in 1974 when, during the Charity Shield against Leeds he and Billy Bremner exchanged blows and were both sent off. The 11-match ban was excessive and Keegan seriously thought about quitting the game but new boss Bob Paisley talked him out of it. That day at Wembley highlighted the tenacious nature of Keegan who despite his 5ft 7in frame was never bullied into submission.

By 1977 he had become a huge star and left for Germany citing a hunger for new challenges. Some fans thought it was more about the money on offer and would soon have new heroes. Keegan, though, had given six great years of his life, had never shirked a challenge and had helped the club begin an unprecedented era of success.

Kevin Keegan fact-file

Appearances	323
Goals	100
England caps while at Liverpool	29

Honours	Season
First Division Championship	1972/73
	1975/76
	1976/77
FA Cup	1974
Uefa Cup	1975/76
European Cup	1976/77
Charity Shield	1974
	1976
Football Writers Player of the Year	1976

— EVERYBODY NEEDS GOOD NEIGHBOURS —

Come matchday, there may be no love lost between the two teams but when it comes to buying and selling personnel, Liverpool have done more deals with Everton than any other club. No fewer than 29 players have made the move across Stanley Park. The first was in 1892, Liverpool's inaugural season when Duncan McLean joined the newly formed club. Here are the other 28 to have crossed the divide:

Blue to red:

Player	Date
Tom Wyllie	September 1892
Patrick Gordon	September 1893
John Whitehead	March 1894
Fred Geary	May 1895
Abraham Hartley	December 1897
David Murray	August 1904
Don Sloan	May 1908
Tom Gracie	February 1912
Harold Uren	February 1912
Bill Lacey	February 1912
Arthur Berry	June 1912
Frank Mitchell	December 1919
Thomas Johnson	March 1934
Jack Balmer	May 1935
Ted Hartill	January 1936
John Heydon	January 1949
Tony McNamara	December 1957
David Hickson	November 1959
Nick Barmby	July 2000
Abel Xavier	January 2002

Red to blue:

Player	Date
Dick Forshaw	March 1927
Jimmy Payne	April 1956
John Morrissey	September 1962
Kevin Sheedy	May 1982
David Johnson	August 1982
Alan Harper	June 1983
Peter Beardsley	August 1991
Gary Ablett	January 1992

— GREAT GAFFERS: BOB PAISLEY (1974–83) —

In 2007 a petition reached 10 Downing Street requesting that Bob Paisley be posthumously knighted. Much to the disappointment of the thousands who had signed the petition, the honours system doesn't allow for posthumous knighthoods but Paisley himself wouldn't have minded one bit. He wasn't one for pomp and ceremony. "Bob get a knighthood?" laughed Ian St John. "He'd turn up at the Palace in his top hat, slippers and the *Daily Mirror* rolled up in his back pocket."

Having retired as a player in 1954, Paisley was club physio, trainer and coach before he reluctantly became manager in 1974. The board thought he was the natural choice to succeed Shankly but Paisley, who saw himself as some sort of 'buffer', had to be cajoled into accepting the post.

Paisley was the cheese to Shankly's chalk. Shankly loved the limelight, Paisley shied away from it; the Scot had a way with words, Paisley often seemed lost for them. "I'll let my team do the talking," he quipped. At first it seemed the side's eloquence had gone with Shankly as they went trophyless in 1974/75 but Paisley was finding his feet, making his own tweaks and soon success would follow. Phil Neal was signed, Terry McDermott came in. Ray Kennedy, signed on the day Shankly resigned, was moved from centre-forward to midfield and suddenly Paisley had a team that would put even Shankly's in the shade.

The title, along with the Uefa Cup, was reclaimed in 1976. However, that magnificent achievement would pale into near insignificance the following season as Paisley's team (and that's what it now was) won another title, just missed out on the Double with a cup final defeat to Manchester United, before travelling to Rome for their first European Cup final where they would face German champions Borussia Monchangladbach. It was here that Paisley was in his element. In his team talk he told the players that the last time he was in Rome, it was in a tank liberating the place. The dressing-room erupted with laughter, the disappointment of Wembley was forgotten and the team put in a fine performance to win 3–1 and bring the cup to Liverpool.

Paisley spent that night in his hotel room, drinking cola (he liked a drink but he wanted to stay sober that night so he could savour and remember every moment) and talking football with his staff and the German captain Bertie Vogts.

The low key celebration was typical of the man. The following year he retained the European Cup and went on to win 13 major trophies in nine seasons. In 1981 he became the only manager in history to win three European Cups but it didn't change him. He remained football's quiet man; he would often forget the words he wanted to use and replace them with his own word, 'Doins'. So it was "Doins on the right wing is no good and his mate, how's your father, is even worse."

In 1982 Paisley decided that enough was enough, he would manage for one last season and call it a day. Another title was won, as was a third consecutive League Cup. After the last of these triumphs, against Manchester United, his players showed how important he was to them by ushering him up the steps at Wembley to become the first manager to collect a trophy at the stadium.

Paisley was offered a role as director at the club and when Kenny Dalglish was appointed as manager in 1986, he played a big role in helping his best-ever signing settle into the job. A massive presence at Anfield, Paisley was diagnosed with Alzheimer's and sadly died in 1996.

Bob Paisley fact-file

Games in charge	535

Honours	Season
Charity Shield	1974
First Division Championship	1975/76
Uefa Cup	1975/76
Charity Shield	1976
First Division Championship	1976/77
European Cup	1976/77
Charity Shield	1977*
European Cup	1977/78
First Division Championship	1978/79
Charity Shield	1979
First Division Championship	1979/80
Charity Shield	1980
League Cup	1980/81
European Cup	1980/81
League Cup	1981/82
First Division Championship	1981/82
Charity Shield	1982
League Cup	1982/83
First Division Championship	1982/83

*Shared trophy

— A KING, NORTH AND SOUTH
OF THE BORDER —

When, on November 26th 1984, Kenny Dalglish scored at Ipswich, he became the first player to score 100 goals in both the Scottish and English leagues with just two clubs. Neil Martin had scored 100 goals in both countries but his came for Alloa, Queen of the South, Hibernian, Sunderland, Coventry and Nottingham Forest. Dalglish is also the first player to win all three domestic honours in both Scotland and England.

— 2005 MIRACLE STATS —

Here's a few numbers for you to ponder regarding Liverpool's 2005 Champions League victory:

350–1	The odds on Liverpool lifting the cup being offered by some online betting sites at half-time.
20,000	The number of flags and hats commemorating the 2005 final that were sold in Liverpool on the day of the match.
30%	The amount by which calls to Liverpool's emergency services were reduced for the duration of the game.

— BRIDGE OF SIGHS —

For all of the club's recent European success over Chelsea, when it comes to winning at their place, Liverpool haven't exactly enjoyed good times. Liverpool were the first visitors to Stamford Bridge. The Reds came down to London for a friendly against the new club on Monday September 4th 1905 and lost 4–0.

Since then they have had mixed fortunes at the Bridge. In 1978 and 1982, Chelsea knocked Liverpool, European champions on both occasions, out of the FA Cup. However Liverpool, aided by player-manager Kenny Dalglish, famously won the league title there in 1986. But having won there again in 1989, Liverpool have since managed just one victory at Chelsea in all competitions; Bruno Cheyrou's effort the difference in a 2004 Premiership fixture.

No wonder famous Red Elvis Costello wrote the song, '(I Don't Want to Go To) Chelsea'.

— SPOT ON JAN —

No one has scored more goals from the penalty spot for Liverpool than 'Great Dane', Jan Molby. Having arrived from Ajax in 1984, Molby went on to make 281 appearances, scoring 60 goals, 42 of them from 12 yards. Molby first showed his penalty prowess in a league game at Anfield on September 28th 1985. That day he scored two spot-kicks in a 4–1 win over Tottenham and, with usual penalty expert Phil Neal finally leaving later that season, he soon became the club's regular penalty taker.

In November 1986 Molby scored a hat-trick of penalties against Coventry City in a League Cup tie and in December 1993, again in the League Cup, he scored against Wimbledon at Anfield to beat Phil Neal's club record of 38 successful penalties. He went on to get three more before leaving the club in 1996.

Here are Liverpool's top five penalty takers of all time:

Player	Penalties scored
Jan Molby	42
Phil Neal	38
Billy Liddell	35
Tommy Smith	22
Robbie Fowler	20

— TOTTENHAM PAY THE PENALTY —

When it comes to scoring penalties, no club has had to endure more spot-kick woes against Liverpool than Tottenham. The Reds have managed 18 penalties against Spurs over the years, two more than the 16 they've scored past Manchester City.

Here are the five clubs to have seen the most Liverpool penalties put past them:

Club	Penalties scored
Tottenham	18
Everton	17
Manchester City	16
Manchester United	16
Nottingham Forest	15

— THE SHANKLY GATES —

On August 26th 1982 at the Anfield Road end, Liverpool Football Club unveiled the Shankly Gates in honour of the man who had made them great. Unlocked for the first time by Shankly's widow, Nessie, the gates include a Scottish flag, a Scottish thistle, the Liverpool badge and the words 'You'll Never Walk Alone'.

— GET WARM, GEOFF —

At the start of the 1965/66 season, substitutes were finally given the green light by the Football League. They could only be used in the event of an injury and Liverpool took advantage of the new ruling on September 15th 1965. Losing 1–0 at home to West Ham, Bill Shankly was forced to replace the injured Chris Lawler and so on went Geoff Strong, Liverpool's first ever substitute. He equalised and ensured a 1–1 draw.

— MATCH OF THE DAY —

"Welcome to *Match of the Day*, the first of a weekly series on BBC Two. This afternoon we are in Beatleville."

With those words, uttered by Ken Wolstenholme on August 22nd 1964, an English institution was born. The first ever *Match of the Day* brought highlights of Arsenal's visit to the champions of England, Liverpool.

Twenty thousand viewers tuned in and it was Roger Hunt who scored the first goal on the then Saturday early evening show. Gordon Wallace grabbed another two and the Reds ran out 3–2 winners.

Liverpool were also involved when *Match of the Day* broadcast its first ever colour transmission on November 15th 1969. This time West Ham were the guests and again Bill Shankly's men ran out winners, goals from Chris Lawler and Bobby Graham securing a 2–0 victory.

— RUSHIE'S UNITED JINX —

For all his goals, for all the trophies those goals brought and, of course, for all the times he broke Everton fans' hearts, Ian Rush is a legend, but for a while there was one team that were proving to be his Achilles heel. In his first stint at the club between 1980 and 1987, Ian Rush failed to score against Manchester United and having returned to Anfield in 1988 it seemed he still couldn't manage it.

Then, on April 26th 1992, United came to Anfield having to avoid defeat to stay in the championship race. In the first half, Rush latched onto a pass in typical fashion, moved into the box and stroked the ball past Peter Schmeichel. Liverpool won 2–0 and United had lost the league to Leeds. The following season Rush scored at Old Trafford in a 2–2 draw making him the club's all-time leading scorer. The jinx was well and truly over.

— ALDO KNOWS BEST? —

While all those around him were losing their heads as Liverpool moved agonisingly closer to their penalty shoot-out victory in Istanbul, John Aldridge kept his cool and passed on his professional knowledge. Co-commentating for Liverpool's Radio City, Aldridge watched as Andrei Shevchenko placed the ball on the spot and prepared to take a penalty that he had to score if his team were to stay in the match. "He'll score," said Aldridge. "He's a good player him."

— WE PLEDGE ALLEGIANCE TO THE FLAG? —

Tuesday February 6th 2007; two businessmen called Tom Hicks and George Gillett Jr are unveiled at Anfield as Liverpool's new owners. Both have a successful background in running sports clubs (sorry, franchises) but up until now their sports have involved pucks, catching mitts and shoulder pads. For now, Liverpool Football Club has gone all American but even the most sceptical Kopites shouldn't despair, the club has long had a connection with the good ol' US of A:

- In a wartime match played in March 1943, Liverpool striker Johnny Shafto made a guest appearance for Southampton against the U.S Army. The Saints won 11–0 and Shafto got six goals.
- In the summer of 1946, Liverpool went on tour to the US. With the war not long over and the Football League set to resume in August, Liverpool's forward thinking chairman William McConnell was concerned that rationing and the poor food supplies in Britain would take their toll on his athletes. His idea, why not travel across the Atlantic? There they would play in ten matches in ten cities, bond as a squad and most importantly gorge themselves on T-bone steaks, fresh eggs and orange juice. It worked. Liverpool won all ten games, attracted thousands of supporters to all their games and took home plenty of nylon stockings – in short supply back home – for their wives. They went on to win the title that season.
- In 1948 Liverpool once more toured the US. There they played the Brooklyn Wanderers whose centre-half, Joe Cadden caught their eye. Liverpool immediately offered him a contract and Cadden became the first player to move to Anfield from America. He made just four appearances before leaving for Grimsby Town in 1952.
- In 1950, Liverpool centre half Laurie Hughes was part of England's World Cup team that incredibly lost 1–0 to the US.
- In 1964, Bill Shankly took Liverpool on tour to America. Shankly was a huge fan of Hollywood gangster movies – Jimmy Cagney was a hero – but once across the Atlantic he couldn't quite get to grips with American ways. He refused to change the time on his watch, "No Yank is going to tell me what the time is," he told his assistant Bob Paisley. All in all the culture clash was too much for him. One travelling journalist told of how Shankly, "could not understand a country in which nobody had heard of Tom Finney."
- Despite Shankly's homesickness, he did use a trip to Chicago on that tour to ensure that a guide took him to the exact spot where the Valentine's Day Massacre took place.

- On that same tour in 1964, the Liverpool squad – who had just become champions of England – made an appearance on *The Ed Sullivan Show*.
- In May 1976, to celebrate the US bicentenary, Team America – a hybrid side of players taking part in the North American Soccer League – played two 'internationals' against England and Brazil. Liverpool's very own Tommy Smith, playing for the Tampa Bay Rowdies in the summer months, played against his home nation as did Bobby Moore who actually captained the side. England won 3–1.
- In 1999, Liverpool legend Steve Nicol moved to the US to become player-coach at the Boston Bulldogs. He remained there until 2002 before taking over New England Revolution, leading the club to the Major League Soccer Cup that season and winning the MLS Coach of the Year award. At the time of writing he was still at Revolution but his name has been touted as a possible future coach of the US national team.
- In 2007, Liverpool joined forces with the Long Island Junior Soccer League in New York. The LISL has been going since 1996 and is now one of the largest youth leagues in America and the first to form an affiliation with a European club. Steve Heighway orchestrated the move before he left the academy and the alliance will see LISL players get the chance to come to Liverpool while their coaches in the States will also get guidance from Liverpool's coaching staff.

— NORTH AMERICAN REDS —

A team of Liverpool stars who also played across the Pond:

1. Bruce Grobbelaar (Vancouver Whitecaps)
2. Gary Ablett (Long Island Rough Riders)
3. Alec Lindsey (Oakland)
4. Steve Nicol (Boston Bulldogs)
5. Joe Cadden (Brooklyn Wanderers)
6. Tommy Smith (Tampa Bay Rowdies)
7. Steve Heighway (Minnesota Kicks)
8. David Fairclough (Toronto Blizzard)
9. David Johnson (Tulsa Roughnecks)
10. Peter Beardsley (Vancouver Whitecaps)
11. Howard Gayle (Dallas Sidekicks)

— RED LEGENDS: STEVEN GERRARD —

Anfield's modern-day hero (and friends)

When Steven Gerrard powered that last minute equaliser past West Ham's Shaka Hislop to take the 2006 FA Cup final into extra-time, he summoned more energy to run and take the plaudits from the delirious fans behind the goal. Amid the bedlam, he turned his back and pointed to the name on his shirt. Like the fans needed reminding.

This was the man who had scored a last gasp goal to keep the team in the Champions League in December 2004. This was the man who a few months later started the remarkable comeback in Istanbul. This was the man who had become a modern day hero at Anfield. A player who drove himself and his team forward, and is now in the upper echelons of Liverpool legends.

Steven Gerrard grew up supporting the club he now captains and was given his debut in 1998 when he came on as a substitute for Vegard Heggam against Blackburn. His ability immediately stood out and while many of his early forays in the team were at right back, Gerrard was clearly a footballer who would soon be moved up field where he could do most damage.

Kevin Keegan picked him for his Euro 2000 squad and it was the following season that he truly stamped his authority on his club side. Gerrard was instrumental in the treble of 2000/01, scoring brilliant goals (his effort against Manchester United at Anfield was voted the club's best-ever Premiership goal by the fans) and giving the first taste of just how he can dominate a football match.

Gerrard was made captain in 2003, the skipper's armband taking its place on his sleeve, next to his heart. There have been problems, of course. Twice Gerrard nearly left for Chelsea, twice he was convinced otherwise and now it looks like he could be at the club for the rest of his career. He's still hungry though, plays every game like it's his last and has become the heartbeat of the team.

When things go wrong, Gerard wears the scowl of an angry fan, when things go right his joy knows no bounds. That joy was, of course, never on show more than in Istanbul in 2005. Gerarrd's looping header hauled Liverpool back into the match, his surging run won them the penalty to make it 3–3. It was his defining moment in red, but I'd whisper that if I were you. Gerrard wants more, he always does, and that's why the fans love him.

Steven Gerrard fact-file

Appearances	483
Goals	120
England caps while at Liverpool	73

Honours	Season
FA Cup	2001
	2006
League Cup	2000/01
	2002/03
European Cup	2004/05
Uefa Cup	2000/01
Charity Shield	2001
	2006
PFA Player of the Year	2006
PFA Young Player of the Year	2001
Football Writers' Footballer of the Year	2009

— A SHORT WORD FROM OUR SPONSORS —

In 1979, Liverpool became the first British team to have a shirt sponsor. Japanese electronic giants Hitachi plastered their name on the strip until 1982 before Crown Paints stepped in. In 1988 it was the turn of Italian home appliance company Candy before the current sponsor Carlsberg got the job in 1992.

— LIVERPOOL'S TOP SCORERS —

Liverpool's top goalscorers in the various competitions:

Competition	Player	Number of goals
League	Roger Hunt	245
FA Cup	Ian Rush	39
League Cup	Ian Rush	48
Europe	Michael Owen	22

— JACK'S MAGIC TRIPLE —

In the first season after the Second World War, Liverpool striker Jack Balmer became the first and only man to score three successive league hat-tricks. The first came on November 9th 1946 at home to Portsmouth, the following Saturday he scored four at Derby before grabbing another three at home to Arsenal on November 23rd 1946,

— THE ORIGINAL LIVERPOOL FC —

When in 1892 the new football club based at Anfield was waiting to start its footballing life, a problem emerged over the club's new name. The city's main rugby team was also called Liverpool FC and they immediately made complaints that the name couldn't be replicated by the new football team. John Houlding agreed that there would be potential confusion and added the word Association to the new title, making the Liverpool Association Football Club. Liverpool Football Club (the rugby version) was formed in 1871 making it the oldest open rugby club in the world. In 1986, they merged with St Helens.

— THAT'S JUST GREEDY —

On 34 occasions, Liverpool players have gone on to bag more than three goals in one match. They are:

Player	Date	Opposition	Goals	Score
John Miller	Dec 3rd 1892	Fleetwood Rovers	5	7–0
George Allan	Sep 28th 1895	Port Vale	4	5–1
George Allan	Feb 18th 1896	Rotherham Town	4	10–0
Andy McGuigan	Jan 4th 1902	Stoke City	5	7–0
Sam Raybould	Dec 6th 1902	Grimsby Town	4	9–2
Robert Robinson	Oct 1st 1904	Leicester City	4	4–0
Jack Parkinson	Apr 20th 1910	Nottingham Forest	4	7–3
Fred Pagnam	Oct 31st 1914	Tottenham	4	7–2
Dick Forshaw	Oct 18th 1924	Sheffield United	4	4–1
William Devlin	Oct 1st 1927	Portsmouth	4	8–2
Gordon Hodgson	Feb 14th 1931	Sheffield W	4	5–3
Harold Barton	Jan 23rd 1932	Chesterfield	4	4–2
Gordon Hodgson	Mar 17th 1934	Birmingham	4	4–1
Fred Howe	Sep 7th 1935	Everton	4	6–0
Jack Balmer	Nov 16th 1946	Derby	4	4–1
Albert Stubbins	Mar 6th 1948	Huddersfield	4	4–0
Louis Bimpson	Sep 19th 1953	Burnley	4	4–0
John Evans	Sep 15th 1954	Bristol Rovers	5	5–3
Billy Liddell	Dec 25th 1954	Ipswich Town	4	6–2
John Evans	Mar 12th 1955	Bury	4	4–3
Roger Hunt	Dec 26th 1963	Stoke City	4	6–1
Alf Arrowsmith	Jan 4th 1964	Derby	4	5–0
Tony Hateley	Feb 19th 1968	Walsall	4	5–2
Ian Rush	Nov 6th 1982	Everton	4	5–0
Ian Rush	Oct 29th 1983	Luton Town	5	6–0
Ian Rush	Apr 7th 1984	Coventry City	4	5–0
Steve McMahon	Sep 23rd 1986	Fulham	4	10–0
Dean Saunders	Sep 18th 1991	Kuusysi Lahti	4	6–1
Ian Rush	Sep 16th 1992	Apollon Limassol	4	6–1

Robbie Fowler	Oct 5th 1993	Fulham	5	5–0
Robbie Fowler	Sep 23rd 1995	Bolton	4	5–2
Robbie Fowler	Dec 14th 1996	Middles-brough	4	5–1
Michael Owen	Oct 24th 1998	Nottingham Forest	4	5–1
Michael Owen	Apr 26th 2003	West Brom	4	6–0

— CARRA'S TURKISH PEP-TALK —

After 120 minutes of gruelling football in the 2005 Champions League final Jamie Carragher had played himself into the ground. His cramp-inducing lunges had helped keep Milan out and now, with his socks around his tired ankles, he could at last have a rest. Well almost. Carragher still had something to do and that was to have a quick word in the ear of his goalkeeper, Jerzey Dudek, who was preparing for a penalty shoot-out and for what would turn into the most important few minutes of his working life. Carragher was aware that Jerzey Dudek was a nice guy and things needed to be said before the kicks began.

"Before we got going I ran over to Jerzey and gave him a pep talk," recalled Carragher. "I don't care what you call it, cheating, gamesmanship, I just wanted to win the European Cup and I told him to do his best to put them off. Jerzey is a dead nice fella, probably too nice, and I knew he'd be dead courteous to them and shake their hands. I said, 'Don't worry about them. You don't know them do you? Put them off lad.'"

Jerzey seemed to get the message as his goalkeeping heroics enabled Liverpool to win the trophy for a fifth time.

— STEVIE G'S PRESSURE TACTICS —

Aged 14, Steven Gerrard went for trials at Manchester United. It was, he has since admitted, only a ploy to pressurise Liverpool into offering him a contract.

— MR WHIPPY GIVES CHASE —

After victory over Real Madrid in the 1981 European Cup final, Liverpool returned to the city and paraded the trophy in an open-top bus in front of thousands of their jubilant fans.

The players and their wives took the applause while occasionally helping themselves from the crates of beer and bottles of wine on board the bus. However, as the bus slowly trudged through the throng the call of nature became hard to ignore. For the boys, there were buckets that could be used but for the girls it was little bit more awkward. Skipper Phil Thompson's wife Marge, was desperate and with the bus reaching the corner of Queens Drive and Utting Avenue towards Anfield, Thompson saw his chance and suggested that he and his wife jump off the bus, ask a local homeowner for the use of their toilet and then board the bus.

Thompson's wife, though, took her time and by the time they came out of the house the bus was disappearing up the road. Thompson once more thought quickly and seeing an ice cream van, he quickly hailed it and asked for a lift. Fine, the driver told them, but they'd have to climb in through the hatch. So there was the captain of the European Champions and his wife climbing up into an ice cream van through the hatch and then chasing their team bus. They finally rejoined the party amid some strange looks.

"Where have you been?" asked the players. Thompson replied, "For a number one, a number two and a ninety-nine!"

— THE BOOT ROOM —

When Bill Shankly arrived at Liverpool in December 1959 he knew right away he had to turn the club around. He also, however, had the nous to realise that there were men there behind the scenes who were well worth holding on to.

The physio and trainer Bob Paisley, the hard-as-nails coach Reuben Bennett and reserve team coach Joe Fagan were all known to the new boss. He had played against Paisley and Fagan (he had tried to sign the latter while manager at Grimsby), and Bennett had worked with Shankly's brother Bob at Dundee.

He told them he wanted them all by his side, he wanted loyalty and he wanted what they did together to be solely for the success of Liverpool Football Club. Shankly got on with his visionary plans for the club from the manager's office while Fagan, Bennett and Paisley used a little cubby hole off the main corridor at Anfield, near the dressing-rooms, for their meetings.

The boots were kept in this small room but with the use of some old beer crates, the men found impromptu seats. The crates had come from a Paul Orr, who had managed an amateur team called Guinness Export, and Liverpool had allowed their players to receive treatment at the club. As a thank you, Orr sent a number of crates of Guinness to the club and the empty crates now constituted the room's only furniture.

Shankly himself stayed out of the boot room, feeling that this was the place for his staff to mull things over, to right wrongs and to sometimes ply opposing managers and coaches with beer, scotch and charm. Just enough to get whatever information they might need from them. The original boot room was born. Legend would make it famous and others would be charged with keeping that legend alive, but it was Messrs Paisley, Fagan and Bennett who were the first to open its hallowed but slightly grubby doors.

The boot room played a vital part in the life of the club until 1993, when manager Graeme Souness had it demolished.

— CLEVER DICKS —

On April 9th 1994, Julian Dicks scored a penalty at Anfield in a 1–0 win over Ipswich. Little did he or the fans know that his strike would be the last Liverpool goal ever scored in front of the old terraced Kop as the Reds failed to find the net in their final two home games of the season.

— A LIVER-BIRD UPON MY CHEST —

What exactly is a Liver-bird? Like all good myths that question offers many answers. It is said that when, in 1207, King John granted the small fishing port of Liverpool (or Lerpool as it was then known) a city charter, his seal included an eagle. However, after this original seal was lost in 1644 when the city was held under siege during the English Civil War, the copy was so unskilfully recreated that the bird on the new seal looked more like a cormorant.

Another school of thought is that the people of the city were so intent on creating something original to symbolise Liverpool that they created the Liver-bird, a cross between an eagle and a cormorant. The vegetation in the mouth of the bird is thought to be seaweed.

Whatever the truth, the bird is now inextricably linked to the city. Not only has it been Liverpool Football Club's symbol since their formation in 1892, two of the birds have also sat on top of the Liver building since 1911. It was said (probably by Everton fans) that Liverpool would never win the FA Cup until the birds flew away. Strangely in 1965 when Liverpool finally won the cup, the birds had been taken down to be cleaned.

— THE BADGE —

Liverpool's club crest hasn't changed much over the years with the Liver-bird always very prominent. To celebrate the club's centenary in 1992, the badge was changed to incorporate the Shankly Gates. Then, in 1993, two eternal flames (representing the flame which burns at the Hillsborough Memorial) were added to the side of the main crest.

— THE HILLSBOROUGH JUSTICE CAMPAIGN —

On April 15th 1989, 96 football fans went to see a football match and didn't come home. Almost two decades on and those who lost loved ones, those who were there and those who today are still traumatised by the events at Hillsborough continue to seek justice and to set the record straight for those who so tragically lost their lives that day in Sheffield. For more details of their campaign, log on to: http://www.contrast.org/hillsborough/

— JOCKY'S ARRIVAL —

In May 1977, while Liverpool fans everywhere were still nursing massive hangovers after the club's first European Cup victory in Rome, Bob Paisley made another shrewd (some might even argue the shrewdest) move into the transfer market. For £100,000 Paisley signed Partick Thistle's Alan Hansen, a future captain who would go on to win eight titles, three European Cups, four League Cups and two FA Cups. *SHOOT* magazine reported the signing with the headline "Liverpool's Six-Figure Mystery Man" and ran a quote from Hansen himself: "I'm really looking forward to life as a Liverpool player and I'm determined not to let them down." Alan, you certainly didn't do that.

— MODERN FOOTBALLERS PLAY TOO MANY GAMES? —

In the 1983/84 season Liverpool won a unique treble of League Championship, League Cup and European Cup. They were knocked out of the FA Cup in the fourth round and played Manchester United in the Charity Shield. In total the team played 67 games and three of the players played every minute of every one of them. Bruce Grobbelaar, Alan Kennedy and Alan Hansen didn't miss a second. Sammy Lee started every game but was substituted in a league game against Everton. Those 67 games played is a Liverpool record for one season.

— RAY'S SAFE —

*Ray Clemence kept a clean sheet in more than half
of his games for Liverpool*

No other Liverpool goalkeeper has kept more clean sheets than Ray Clemence. Between 1969 and 1981, in 666 appearances for the club, Clemence kept the score blank an incredible 335 times. Clemence's 28 clean sheets in the 1978/79 season remain a record while the record of conceding just 16 league goals that same season was finally beaten by Chelsea's Peter Cech who let in only 15 goals during the 2004/05 campaign.

— GERMANY 1, LIVERPOOL 5 —

On September 1st 2001, England travelled to Munich to play Germany in a vital qualifying match for the following summer's World Cup finals in Japan. The group remained tight but when Germany took a sixth-minute lead, things looked bleak for Sven Goran Eriksson's men. Step forward England's Liverpool contingent. Michael Owen equalised after good work from Nick Barmby, and Steven Gerrard made it 2–1 just before half-time. The second half turned into a rout with Michael Owen completing his hat-trick before Emile Heskey put the finishing touches to an incredible night.

— HAT-TRICK HEROES —

The first Liverpool player to score a hat-trick was John Miller on October 15th 1892 in an FA Cup qualifying round at Nantwich in front of just 700 people. Since then plenty more have gone on to grab the match ball. Here are some hat-trick facts:

- Gordon Hodgson has scored more hat-tricks for Liverpool than any other player. The South African-born forward managed 17 between 1925 and 1935.
- Ian Rush scored Liverpool's first league hat-trick to be seen live on television. Rush got three goals against Aston Villa at Villa Park on January 20th 1984.
- Robbie Fowler boasts the quickest Premiership hat-trick ever. On August 28th 1994, Fowler got three goals in four minutes and 33 seconds to ensure a 3–0 win over Arsenal at Anfield.
- All hat-tricks are welcomed but some are just plain unexpected. On two occasions, Liverpool players you wouldn't think of as prolific managed to grab hat-tricks. Take a bow Gary Gillespie (three goals v Birmingham, April 26th 1986) and Steve Staunton (three goals v Wigan in the League Cup, October 4th 1989).
- Roger Hunt holds the record for the most hat-tricks scored in a single season. The 1961/62 campaign in which Liverpool won promotion to the First Division saw Hunt score an unprecedented five hat-tricks. They came in the following games:

Date	Opposition	Score
Aug 26th 1961	Leeds United	5–0
Oct 14th 1961	Walsall	6–1
Nov 25th 1961	Swansea	5–0
Feb 10th 1962	Bury	3–0
Feb 24th 1962	Middlesbrough	5–1

— EUROPE'S FINEST —

In 2001 Michael Owen became the first and to date only Liverpool player to win the European Footballer of the Year (or Ballon d'Or) award. That year Owen's goals had helped Liverpool win the FA Cup, the League Cup and Uefa Cup. He had also scored a fine hat-trick for England in Germany.

— PFA REDS —

Liverpool players have won the Professional Footballer's Association Player of the Year on five occasions:

Player	Year
Terry McDermott	1980
Kenny Dalglish	1983
Ian Rush	1984*
John Barnes	1988
Steven Gerrard	2006*

Liverpool players have also won the PFA Young Player of the Year award on five occasions:

Player	Year
Ian Rush	1983*
Robbie Fowler	1995
Robbie Fowler	1996
Michael Owen	1998
Steven Gerrard	2001*

*Ian Rush and Steven Gerrard are two of five players that have won both the Young Player and the Player of the Year awards. The other three are Andy Gray, Mark Hughes and Cristiano Ronaldo.

— SCRIBES KNOW BEST —

Since it's formation in 1947, the Football Writers' Association have voted a Liverpool player as their player of the year on 11 occasions – more than any other club. These are the winners:

Player	Year
Ian Callaghan	1974
Kevin Keegan	1976
Emlyn Hughes	1977
Kenny Dalglish	1979
Terry McDermott	1980
Kenny Dalglish	1983
Ian Rush	1984
John Barnes	1988
Steve Nicol	1989
John Barnes	1990
Steven Gerrard	2009

— ENJOY THE GAME, YOUR MAJESTY? —

In 1914, the FA Cup final was attended for the first time by the reigning monarch. George V and his advisors felt that the Royal family had lost touch with its subjects and looked to come up with ways to make the King more accessible to the people.

By 1914, football had become by far the most popular spectator sport in the country and while the official attendance for the final held at Crystal Palace in London was 72,778, it is thought that far closer to 100,000 crammed into the stadium. They, like their King, had come to see Liverpool take on Burnley.

It was Liverpool's first cup final and thousands travelled down by train for the match for what they hoped would be a first taste of glory. With it being an all north-west affair, the King took a prudent PR decision and wore the red rose of Lancashire in his jacket lapel. Alas, Liverpool lost to a 58th minute goal but no matter, the team arrived back by train and were greeted by thousands of commiserating but proud fans.

— TRY STOPPING THIS HUNT —

The 1961/62 season was to be a triumphant one for Liverpool and their fairly new manager Bill Shankly. His new signings all in place, promotion to the First Division would prove easy, especially with his star striker Roger Hunt in prolific form. Hunt played 41 league games that season and scored 41 goals. No striker since has scored as many for the Reds in a single league season.

— MILLENNIUM MAGIC —

In all, Liverpool played seven games at the Millennium Stadium in Cardiff whilst Wembley was being rebuilt. They won six of these and lost just once:

Date	Opposition	Competition	Score
Feb 25th 2001	Birmingham	League Cup final	1–1
		(Won 5–4 on pens)	
May 12th 2001	Arsenal	FA Cup final	2–1
Aug 12th 2001	Manchester United	Community Shield	2–1
Mar 2nd 2003	Manchester United	League Cup final	2–0
Feb 27th 2005	Chelsea	League Cup final	2–3
May 13th 2006	West Ham United	FA Cup final	3–3
		(Won 3–1 on pens)	
Aug 13th 2006	Chelsea	Community Shield	2–1

— MEET THE OWNERS: TOM HICKS —

- Tom Hicks was born in 1946 in Texas, the son of a Texas Radio Station owner.
- In 1968 Hicks received a Bachelors degree in Finance from the University of Texas.
- Hicks' first business interests saw him follow in his father's footsteps into the world of radio and media.
- In 1988 Hicks' company bought several soft drink makers including Dr Pepper and 7Up.
- Hicks' business interests range from oil, electronics in China and pet food in Argentina.
- The Tom Hicks Elementary School in Frisco, Texas was named after the businessman after he donated land to the existing school.
- Hicks has contributed hundreds of thousands of dollars in donations to fellow Texan and friend George W. Bush's political campaigns.
- In 1995 Hicks bought the National Hockey League's (NHL) Dallas Stars for $82 million. Since then the Stars have won seven Division Championships, three Western Conference crowns and enjoyed two consecutive trips to the Stanley Cup finals, winning the massive trophy outright in 1999.
- In 1998 Hicks branched out into baseball, buying the Texas Rangers for $250 million. Since his arrival the Rangers have won the American league West Division in 1998 and 1999 but are yet to win the World Series.
- Hicks' company also owns the Mesquite Championship Rodeo in Texas. Hicks bought the Rodeo in 1999 and since his stewardship, attendances have risen to 200,000. It is watched by 8.3m people on American television making it the most watched rodeo in the world.
- Hicks is married with six children and lives in Preston Hollow, a neighbourhood in North Dallas.

— WE WAS ROBBED! —

At the end of the Liverpool's first season in existence, the owners of the new club would have had to spend that bit more cash on a healthy supply of silver polish. The Lancashire League was won easily, as was the Liverpool Senior Cup, Everton the beaten finalists. The trophies were proudly put on show in a local shop window only to be stolen shortly after. The club were held responsible and had to pay £127 to replace them.

— RED LEGENDS: EMLYN HUGHES —

"It's debatable if there's a better player in the game," Bill Shankly once said of Emlyn Hughes. "Oh, he's got everything. Ability, guts, he's quick, good in the air. You name it, he has it." High praise indeed and it was that all-round ability that allowed Hughes to excel for so long at Liverpool, to play at full-back, centre-back and in midfield and to become one of the most popular players amongst the fans.

Hughes arrived at Anfield from Blackpool in 1967, having made only 31 appearances for the Bloomfield Road club but his signature was a sought after one, and Shankly was adamant that he had once more done good business despite the £65,000 fee.

The son of a British Rugby League player, Hughes was naturally athletic and stood out for his immediate dedication to the cause in a team that, as the swinging sixties drew to an end, was beginning to look a little jaded.

In the last days of the decade, Hughes scored the first goal in a 3–0 win at Goodison (Sandy Brown got his infamous own goal in the same game). Such was the ferocity and enthusiastic nature of his performance that Evertonians gave him the nickname, 'Crazy Horse'. It stuck.

As Shankly morphed his team into new, dynamic form, Hughes was at the hub of that change. Tommy Smith had been made captain after Ron Yeats' departure but midway through the 1973/74 season, Shankly decreed that Hughes was the new man for the job, despite the fact that Smith in the previous campaign had just lifted the League Championship trophy and Uefa Cup.

It was then that Shankly also changed Hughes from a dynamic midfielder into an astute centre half and his partnership with a young Phil Thompson helped the side win that year's FA Cup at Wembley. The great grin on his face as he lifted the cup mirrored that of the fans who cheered his every move. Hughes lost his mentor that summer when Shankly resigned but his leadership continued under Bob Paisley and in 1977, in Rome, the two men led Liverpool to arguably their finest hour.

With Borussia Moenchengladbach beaten 3–1, Hughes walked like an excited schoolboy toward the European Cup. "All I was thinking about was the past teams," he once said. "Players like Ronnie Yeats and Ian St John. It was their efforts that allowed us to win it. As a team we'd done it, but the victory was about the whole club and its efforts over a number of years."

Hughes' efforts were for the team, the club and the fans and so despite lifting the trophy once more at Wembley in 1978, he was aware that it was the right time to go. "Bob knew I was nearing the end of my time. I'd been there for 12 years and it's never nice to be replaced, but it was the correct thing for the team and that was the priority."

Hughes went to Wolves, had a spell as a manager and then a TV star on *Question of Sport*. To Kopites, though, he was the captain, he was 'Crazy Horse', and that is why when he died in 2004 of a brain tumor he was so deeply mourned by fans of all ages.

Emlyn Hughes fact-file
Appearances: 665
Goals: 48
England caps while at Liverpool: 59

Honours	Season
First Division Championship	1972/73
	1975/76
	1976/77
	1978/79
FA Cup	1974
Uefa Cup	1972/73
European Cup	1976/77
	1977/78
Charity Shield	1974
	1976
	1977*
Football Writers' Player of the Year	1977

*Shared

— LIVERPOOL'S FIRST EVER MATCH —

In 1892 Liverpool's application to the Football League was denied and they had to play their first season in the Lancashire League. Before the league term kicked off, though, Liverpool played a friendly at Anfield against Rotherham Town.

The match was scheduled for September 1st at 5.30pm, the exact time that Everton were kicking-off their league campaign at home to Bolton. Liverpool's fledgling board predicted in the local press that, "No better game will be witnessed on any of the plots in the neighbourhood."

Unfortunately, the PR offensive didn't work. Everton drew a crowd of 10,000 that day while Anfield was virtually empty, as Liverpool ran out 7–1 winners.

During the match Liverpool wore the blue-and-white quartered shirts they would use for the next few years. The team was: Ross, Hannah, Mclean, Kelso, McQue, McBride, Wyllie, Smith, Miller, McVean and Kelvin.

— EE AY ADIO, WE WON (AND LOST) THE CUP —

Liverpool have been to 13 FA Cup finals, winning seven and losing six. In fact, their first two trips, in 1914 and 1950, ended in defeat to Burnley and Arsenal respectively.

The Reds finally got their hands on the famous old trophy in 1965, lost to Arsenal again in 1971 before winning it once more in 1974. They then lost (and missed out on the Treble) to Manchester United in 1977. Under Kenny Dalglish the defeat to Wimbledon in 1988 was sandwiched between 1986 and 1989 wins over Everton. The Reds won again in 1992, lost again to United in 1996 before winning it twice in Cardiff in 2001 and 2006.

The full list of Liverpool's FA Cup final appearances is:

Year	Result	Venue
1914	Burnley 1 Liverpool 0	Crystal Palace
1950	Arsenal 2 Liverpool 0	Wembley
1965	Liverpool 2 Leeds 1 (aet)	Wembley
1971	Arsenal 2 Liverpool 1 (aet)	Wembley
1974	Liverpool 3 Newcastle 0	Wembley
1977	Manchester United 2 Liverpool 1	Wembley
1986	Liverpool 3 Everton 1	Wembley
1988	Wimbledon 1 Liverpool 0	Wembley
1989	Liverpool 3 Everton 2 (aet)	Wembley
1992	Liverpool 2 Sunderland 0	Wembley
1996	Manchester United 1 Liverpool 0	Wembley
2001	Liverpool 2 Arsenal 1	Millennium Stadium
2006	Liverpool 3 West Ham 3	Millennium Stadium
	(Won 3–1 on pens)	

— RED ROSE CHAMPIONS —

Liverpool played their first Lancashire League match on September 3rd 1892 in front of just 200 fans at Anfield. Higher Walton were the hapless opponents soundly beaten 8–0, and that's exactly how easy the season continued to be.

Club owner John Houlding had appointed William Barclay and John McKenna as joint managers (Barclay looked after the administration and McKenna kept an eye on team affairs). Under the pair's astute stewardship, Liverpool won 17 of their 22 games, easily becoming champions of Lancashire.

— IT AIN'T OVER TIL IT'S OVER —

"This is finished lad, let's go the pub?" How many poor souls must have uttered those half-time words at the Ataturk Stadium in Istanbul on May 25th 2005. The Reds, 3–0 down, outclassed, supposedly beaten and ready to play out the formalities. We all know what happened next but spare a thought for the fans who upped and left. They aren't alone. Over the years, Liverpool have many times snatched victory from the jaws of defeat, leaving fans throughout the generations sick that they left early.

Other examples of Liverpool comebacks:

Year	Opposition	Deficit	Result
Dec 4th 1909	Newcastle	5–2 down at half-time	Won 6–5
Nov 21st 1970	Everton	2–0 down after 68 minutes	Won 3–2
Sep 29th 1992	Chesterfield	3–0 down after 48 minutes	Drew 4–4
Jan 4th 1994	Manchester United	3–0 down after 24 minutes	Drew 3–3
May 13th 2006	West Ham United	2–0 down after 28 minutes	Drew 3–3*

* Won 3–1 on penalties

— LIVERPOOL'S OLDEST GOALSCORER —

On March 5th 1960, Billy Liddell – making a rare appearance as his career drew to an end – scored the third goal in a 5–1 trouncing of Stoke at Anfield. It was to be his last goal for the club he had so brilliantly served since 1946. At 38 years and 55 days, the brilliant Scotsman is the oldest man ever to score for the Reds.

— THE HILLSBOROUGH MEMORIAL —

Standing next to the Shankly Gates is a memorial to the 96 fans who lost their lives on April 15th 1989 at Hillsborough. Each of those fans' names is engraved in the memorial and an eternal flame means they will never be forgotten. Justice for the 96.

— RED LEGENDS: BILLY LIDDELL —

"Lidellpool, Lidellpool, Lidellpool!"

While Liverpool floundered in the Second Division throughout the 1950s, fans still flocked to Anfield in their tens of thousands. The reason? Billy Liddell. Such was the great Scot's pulling-power that those fans who queued to see him every other week nicknamed their club, 'Liddellpool' in honour of his single-handed efforts.

An accountancy student, Billy Liddell arrived at Anfield aged 17. He was on the verge of making the first team but the Second World War scuppered those plans and despite some wartime appearances he had to wait until 1946, just weeks after being demobbed from the army, before he made his first team debut. That first season back he was a revelation, an electric winger who lit up a football match, even in an era when wonderful wide men were in abundance.

Liddell helped the team to the championship in 1946/47 and became one of the finest players in the league. Despite the prowess of English wingers Tom Finney and Stanley Matthews, Liddell was twice asked to represent Great Britain teams and wherever Liverpool played he was a crowd puller and crowd pleaser.

Early on in the 1950 FA Cup final, Liddell got injured. He manfully soldiered on but without his pace and aggression, Liverpool's attack stuttered and the team lost 2–0 to Arsenal. After that defeat there was a demise in the team's fortunes but Liddell continued to give his all, his skill was never in question but despite clearly being the team's best player, he had no pretensions and mucked in for the cause more than anyone.

It was that attitude that further endeared him to the fans. He continued to work as an accountant; he was teetotal, he was a Methodist preacher on the side, supported many charities and even found time to put in some stints as a hospital radio DJ.

Liddell played at Liverpool until 1961 before retiring and becoming a fan. He died in 2001 but ask those who saw him and they will tell you he is one of the best, if not the best player Liverpool have ever had. Ian Callaghan, the man who replaced Liddell as the club's all-time record appearance maker and who idolised the player from the terraces as a boy, had this to say about him. "In my opinion, Liddell, Keegan and Dalglish were the club's best players ever, but I would put Billy ahead of the other two as being the greatest."

Billy Liddell fact-file

Appearances	537
Goals	229
Scotland caps while at Liverpool	28

Honours	Season
First Division Championship	1946/47

— CAN WE PLAY NOU EVERY WEEK? —

It holds 120,000 of the world's most passionate and intimidating fans. It is home to one of the world's most famous and most respected teams. The greatest coaches in the world have been pleased to leave with a marginal defeat. In short it is one of the world's truly great football arenas, a venue to strike fear into the most competent teams, unless of course you're Liverpool. The Reds have played at the Nou Camp on four occasions, have won twice and are yet to lose. It's easy when you know how:

Date	Competition /Stage	Score
March 30th 1976	Uefa Cup semi-final first leg	1–0
April 5th 2001	Uefa Cup semi-final first leg	0–0
March 13th 2002	Champions League second group stage	0–0
February 21st 2007	Champions League second round, first leg	2–1

— NEAL'S BULGING TROPHY CABINET —

Phil Neal and an old friend

Bob Paisley's first signing in 1974, Phil Neal went on to be the club's most decorated player winning 22 winners' medals. He beats Alan Hansen who won 21. These are Neal's winning gongs:

Year	Competition
1975/76	League Championship
1975/76	Uefa Cup
1976	Charity Shield
1976/77	League Championship
1976/77	European Cup
1977	Charity Shield*
1977	European Super Cup
1977/78	European Cup

1978/79	League Championship
1979	Charity Shield
1979/80	League Championship
1980	Charity Shield
1980/81	League Cup
1980/81	European Cup
1981/82	League Cup
1981/82	League Championship
1982	Charity Shield
1982/83	League Cup
1982/83	League Championship
1983/84	League Cup
1983/84	League Championship
1983/84	European Cup

*Charity Shield shared with Manchester United after 0–0 draw

— SPRINGKOPS —

Liverpool have long had a connection with South Africa. Not only was the Kop End named after a battle over there during the Boer War (see *The Birth of a Legend*, page 14) but the club, through the years, have recruited a number of South African born or bred players. Four of them, Kemp, Riley, Rudham and Grobbelaar were goalkeepers. These are the South African-born players to have played for the Reds:

Name	Seasons	Appearances	Goals
Arthur Riley	1925–1939	338	0
Gordon Hodgson	1925–1936	378	240
WilliamGray	1928–1929	1	0
Lance Carr	1933–1935	33	8
Berry Nieuwenhuys	1933–1947	260	79
Harman Van Den Berg	1937–1940	22	4
Dirk Kemp	1937–1939	33	0
Bob Priday	1946–1949	23	6
Hugh Gerhardi	1952–1953	6	0
Doug Rudham	1954–1960	63	0
Bruce Grobbelaar	1981–1994	627	0
Craig Johnston	1981–1988	268	40
Sean Dundee	1998–1999	5	0
Mark Gonzalez	2006–2007	36	3

— RUSH SCORES, REDS WIN —

Ian Rush scored his first goal for Liverpool on September 30th 1981 in a European Cup tie against Finnish side Oulu Palloseura at Anfield. Rush bagged the fifth in a 7–0 win and for the next six years maintained an incredible record. Every time Liverpool's prolific goal-getter scored, Liverpool were undefeated.

It became a celebrated sequence that wasn't broken until April 5th 1987, the Welshman's last season in his first spell at the club. Rush scored the first goal in the Littlewoods Cup Final at Wembley against Arsenal. The Gunners, though, fought back and won 2–1, breaking Rush's winning streak. Strangely, the following week at Norwich, Rush once more scored but again Liverpool were beaten 2–1.

— LEAGUE, MILK, COLA AND ALE —

Founded in 1961 the League Cup held little interest to Bill Shankly and Liverpool Football Club. In fact it wasn't until the late 1970s that the Reds started taking the competition seriously. They lost to Nottingham Forest in the 1978 final but then went on a winning streak that saw them win four in a row between 1981 and 1984. Since then Liverpool have won the cup again in 1995, 2001 and 2003. The seven times they have lifted the trophy (Liverpool have won it as the League, Milk, Coca-Cola and Worthington Cup) is a record.

The full list of Liverpool's League Cup final appearances:

Year	Result	Venue
1978	Nottingham Forest 0 Liverpool 0	Wembley
1978	Nottingham Forest 1 Liverpool 0 (replay)	Old Trafford
1981	West Ham United 1 Liverpool 1 (aet)	Wembley
1981	Liverpool 2 West Ham United (replay)	Villa Park
1982	Liverpool 3 Tottenham 1 (aet)	Wembley
1983	Liverpool 2 Manchester United 1 (aet)	Wembley
1984	Everton 0 Liverpool 0 (aet)	Wembley
1984	Liverpool 1 Everton 0 (replay)	Maine Road
1987	Arsenal 2 Liverpool 1	Wembley
1995	Liverpool 2 Bolton 1	Wembley
2001	Liverpool 1 Birmingham 1 (5–4 on pens)	Millennium Stadium
2003	Liverpool 2 Manchester United 0	Millennium Stadium
2005	Chelsea 3 Liverpool 2 (aet)	Millennium Stadium

— GREAT GAFFERS: JOE FAGAN —

In the spring of 1983, Bob Paisley addressed an audience in London gathered to honour his illustrious career. "There's a man following me called Fagan – and he doesn't need the help of an Artful Dodger to pick up anything that glitters," he joked.

When Joe Fagan became manager of Liverpool in 1983, he didn't have to settle into the Liverpool way because he had been behind the scenes since 1958. The Liverpool way was very much his way.

A good player, Fagan had actually turned down Liverpool as a youngster worried that local boys (Fagan was a Scouser) would be made scapegoats if things went wrong and instead went on to captain Manchester City. Having become trainer at Rochdale, Liverpool asked him to Melwood to train the players. An integral part of the boot room, Fagan was very popular with the players, providing a useful buffer between them and the manager.

Fagan inherited a squad of players who had won successive titles and was packed with internationals but his achievement in winning three trophies in a season in 1983/84 should not be underestimated. He also added to the squad, recruiting useful players like Michael Robinson, John Wark and Paul Walsh.

Fagan's first trophy was the League Cup (Liverpool's fourth in a row) and another title was won with a win at Notts County in the penultimate match. After the game, Fagan could be seen sweeping the floors of the away dressing room at Meadow Lane before boarding the bus.

Just over two weeks later, Fagan was in the slightly grander surroundings of Rome for the European Cup final against the home side, Roma. It was a massive task to beat the Italians on their own patch but Fagan's team was crammed full of character and battled to silence the crowd before winning the cup on penalties.

Graeme Souness hoisted the famous trophy toward the Roman gods but it was to be his last game before moving to Italy for good. The loss of his midfield general and skipper was a big blow and Fagan's side conceded their league title to Everton. However, with Jan Molby settling into the Souness berth and John Wark providing goals from midfield, Liverpool reached yet another European Cup final, this time at the Heysal stadium in Brussels.

The events of that night cast a cloud over the club, the sport and Fagan himself. He had told his players prior to the match that after the game they could call him Joe again rather than boss but what was supposed to be a joyous night turned into tragedy as 39 fans, most of them Italian, lost their lives. The image of Fagan getting off the plane at Liverpool airport, hunched and in tears, summed up the mood of the day and the club.

Fagan will be remembered for the treble of 1983/84 but his contribution to the Liverpool cause extended well beyond that season of success. Just weeks after Liverpool had achieved yet another treble in 2001, Fagan died at the age of 80.

Joe Fagan fact-file

Games in charge	131

Honours	Season
League Cup	1983/84
First Division Championship	1983/84
European Cup	1983/84

— ANFIELD'S NATIONAL SERVICE —

England's first ever international in the city of Liverpool was played on April 24th 1883, nine years before Liverpool Football Club was formed. The game was against Northern Ireland at Aigburth Park Cricket Club and England won 7–0.

Anfield hosted its first international on March 2nd 1889 when Ireland were beaten 6–1. It was then the home of Everton but ever since and as home of Liverpool, the old ground has hosted seven England matches:

Date	Opponents	Score
March 27th 1905	Wales	3–1
March 13th 1922	Wales	1–0
October 20th 1926	Northern Ireland	3–3
November 18th 1931	Wales	3–1
March 24th 2001	Finland	2–1
April 17th 2002	Paraguay	4–0
May 1st 2006	Uruguay	2–1

England also played Liverpool in two testimonials at Anfield. The first came at the end of the 1983 season when Bobby Robson brought his England side to play against Liverpool for Phil Thompson's testimonial. Then, on May 16th 1988, England visited again for Alan Hansen's testimonial match at Anfield. More than 30,000 fans came along to see Liverpool win 3–2 just two days after losing the FA Cup final to Wimbledon.

— STEVIE WONDER —

Steven Gerrard is the only man ever to score in a League Cup final, an FA Cup final, a Uefa Cup final and a Champions League Cup final. These are the great man's landmark goals:

Date	Competition	Opponents	Goal(s)	Score
May 16th 2001	Uefa Cup	Alaves	1	W5–4
Mar 2nd 2003	League Cup	Manchester United	1	W2–0
May 25th 2005	Champions League	AC Milan	1	D3–3
May 13th 2006	FA Cup	West Ham	2	D3–3

— WHAT'S IN A NUMBER? —

There was a simple, innocent time when players ran out numbered from 1 to 11. Number 2s were right-backs, 7s were strikers, 9s were goalscorers and 12s were substitutes. You knew where you were. Your heroes wore the numbers with distinction. Ian St John and Ian Rush were number 9s, Kevin Keegan and Kenny Dalglish number 7s.

Times change, however. Now goalkeeper Pepe Reina wears number 25, Peter Crouch is number 15. But in these confusing times one unlikely number has bred two true Anfield legends. When he first broke on the scene as a prodigious getter of goals, Robbie Fowler wore the number 23 shirt (the number 23 was made famous the world over by basketball legend Michael Jordan while playing for the Chjicago Bulls). Fowler's legend set in stone, he was given the number 9 jersey when Ian Rush left in 1996. His 23 shirt was then handed to the supposed utility player Jamie Carragher, who to this day wears the shirt with pride. When Carra hangs it up on his dressing-room peg for the last time, perhaps the club should retire the 23 as well – either that or hand it to the next Liverpool-born hopeful!

— A SHANKLY GEM —

November 21st 1970, Anfield. Liverpool have beaten Everton 3–2 in a classic derby match. The Kop stays packed way after the whistle, saluting the team, preparing to gloat at the misfortune of their neighbours. Bill Shankly comes out of the dressing-room to do an interview and hears the Kop still cheering.

"They must be waiting for the other results," says the interviewer.

"Why, were there other games?" says Shanks.

— SHAKIN' ALL OVER —

Liverpool's halcyon years were always built on stability but even the likes of Bill Shankly and Bob Paisley would have been surprised by the steps the club took in the summer of 2000. Huge poles had to be inserted in the two-year-old Anfield Road end after faults in the construction were discovered, thanks largely to 12,000 Glaswegians.

On May 13th 2000, Anfield was packed, noisy and in celebratory mood in honour of Ronnie Moran's testimonial. Liverpool's faithful old retainer was being given his send off in a game against Celtic and as the travelling fans packed into the Anny Road, supporters around the ground noted that they could see that part of the ground 'moving' under the enthusiastic weight of the Celtic fans. Fortunately, reinforcement work was immediately carried out in time for the following season.

— WELL DONE BOSS —

Liverpool managers have won the Manager of the Year award on eleven occasions. Incredibly the great Bill Shankly won it only once, but Paisley made up for lost time and won it six times. Joe Fagan won it once while Kenny Dalglish won it three times. A Liverpool boss hasn't won it since. Over to you, Rafa.

Liverpool's Managers of the Season:

Year	Manager	Trophies won
1973	Bill Shankly	League Championship, Uefa Cup
1976	Bob Paisley	League Championship, Uefa Cup
1977	Bob Paisley	League Championship, European Cup
1979	Bob Paisley	League Championship
1980	Bob Paisley	League Championship
1982	Bob Paisley	League Championship, League Cup
1983	Bob Paisley	League Championship, League Cup
1984	Joe Fagan	League Championship, League Cup, European Cup
1986	Kenny Dalglish	League Championship, FA Cup
1988	Kenny Dalglish	League Championship
1990	Kenny Dalglish	League Championship

The trophy was long sponsored by Bells whisky and, having given so much of the stuff to Bob Paisley over the years, in 1983 they decided to give the great man a commemorative bell instead.

— MAKE UP YOUR MIND UP LADS —

In the 114 years of Merseyside derbies, only two men have scored for both teams. David Johnson scored the only goal for the Blues at Goodison in November 1971, a feat he would repeat, this time in the red of Liverpool on April 5th 1978.

Peter Beardsley got his first Merseyside derby goal in the league game at Anfield on November 1st 1988. Annoyingly, the brilliant little striker, having been sold to them lot across the park, also scored the winner at Goodison in December 1992.

— WINNERS IN RED AND BLUE —

Only one man has won championship-winning medals with both Liverpool and Everton. Dick Forshaw came to Liverpool in 1919. A talented inside-forward he was an ever-present in both title winning seasons of 1922 and 1923. Forshaw moved to Everton in 1927 and won the title in blue in 1928.

Meanwhile, Gary Ablett is the only player to win the FA Cup for both Merseyside clubs. In 1989, Ablett was in the Liverpool team that beat Everton to win the cup. He moved to Everton in 1992 and was part of Joe Royle's 1995 FA Cup-winning side.

— ONE HIT WADDLE —

You may not have heard of one-time Liverpool forward Alan Waddle. Chris's cousin, Waddle played 22 games for Liverpool in the 1970s, scoring just one goal, but what a goal to score.

December 1973 and Liverpool are at Goodison Park toiling away, a goalless draw looking the more than likely result. Then, with just over 20 minutes to go, Alan Waddle, in for the injured John Toshack, nips in and scores a goal. His only goal. Cue Liverpool fans singing, "Waddle, Waddle, Waddle, Quack, Quack, Quack!" Waddle stayed until 1977 and was an unused substitute in Rome when Liverpool won the European Cup that year.

— THE ITALIAN JOB —

On May 13th 2007, just ten days before losing in Athens to AC Milan, Liverpool fielded the first Italian player in their history. Reserve keeper Daniele Padelli, on loan from Sampdoria, kept goal in the last game of the season against Charlton, a 2–2 draw.

— RED LEGENDS: JOHN BARNES —

In early December 1986, Liverpool travelled to Watford's Vicarage Road hoping for three points in the chase to retain their title. Watford were no longer the force they had been when they first came up in the early part of the decade but in John Barnes they had one of the most impressive forwards in the country.

In the second half, with the Hornets already a goal up, Barnes picked up the ball near the centre circle and set off for goal. Despite a boggy pitch the ball clung to his boot, and with a swerve of the hips he mesmerised Alan Hansen and Gary Gillespie before caressing a deft shot past Bruce Grobbelaar. Game over. In the away end there was silence. It was a blow to the title hopes but suddenly and spontaneously there was applause. It was that good a goal, and Barnes was that good a player.

Months later, that applause would turn to wild cheers as Kenny Dalglish captured the signature of John Barnes for £900,000 as part of his new and exciting Liverpool team. With John Aldridge scoring, Peter Beardsley probing and John Barnes bamboozling the opposition, fans were treated to some of the most free-flowing and exciting football they had ever seen. The title was won, Barnes took both Player of the Year awards and despite the FA Cup defeat to Wimbledon the season remains an iconic one.

Barnes had more than won over the fans (who nicknamed him 'Tarmac' – the black Heighway). Some had been sceptical about the move, wondering about his commitment to the cause after he had stalled over his decision, while there was also the issue of how a black player would fare on Merseyside where none had regularly ventured before. Barnes, though, was as smooth off the pitch as on it and even when a banana was thrown his way at Goodison that year, he simply back-heeled it into touch. His talent and his manner smashed down any barriers.

Barnes was part of the squad that in 1989 helped so many grieving families after the tragedy of Hillsborough and then brought the FA Cup home when the business of football once more got under way. The following season was perhaps Barnes' best. Liverpool retained the title in 1990, and Barnes was once more voted the Football Writers' Player of the Year, having scored an impressive 27 goals.

It was to be his last season as a truly dynamic and explosive winger. By the time Graeme Souness was settled into the managerial job, Barnes had suffered a debilitating Achilles tendon injury that would deprive him of that burst of pace, but when Roy Evans took over he was brilliantly deployed as an intelligent deep-lying midfielder, his passing as potent as his dribbling.

As the wise head in Evans' exciting young team, Barnes added a

League Cup winner's medal to his collection of gongs in 1995 but that was that and in 1997, he left for Newcastle. The 1980s had been a special decade for Liverpool, but was there a better sight during those ten years than Barnes beating another downtrodden right back before whipping the ball into the box?

John Barnes fact-file

Appearances	409
Goals	108
England caps while at Liverpool	48

Honours	Season
First Division Championship	1987/88
	1989/90
FA Cup	1989
League Cup	1994/95
Charity Shield	1988
	1989
	1990*
Footballer Writers' Player of the Year	1988
	1990
PFA Player of the Year	1988

*Shared

— JUST FOR LAUGHS* —

Two Scousers are having a pint. One says to the other, "My awl fella died the other day and we spread his ashes at the Kop end."

"Really'" says his mate, an Evertonian. "That doesn't happen at Goodison."

"What happens there?"

We stuff 'em and put 'em back in their seats."

"Really?"

"Yeah. Last week we stuffed my dead uncle and put him in his seat for the match."

"That's amazing."

"You think that's amazing? At half-time he got up and went home."

*Courtesy of Stan Boardman

— TORRES FACTS —

- Fernando Torres started out in football as a goalkeeper. As a young boy he tried to save a shot but the ball hit him in the face and broke two teeth. He immediately changed to a striker.
- Atletico took part in an under-14 tournament called the Nike Cup in 1998. They beat the likes of Juventus, Barcelona, Manchester United and AC Milan to win the trophy and Torres was their star. He was quickly voted the most promising player of that age group in Europe.
- In 2001, aged just 16, Torres became the youngest player ever to play for Atletico. Aged 19, he became the club's youngest ever captain. Torres scored 82 goals for the club in 214 appearances.
- Torres has three tattoos. On the inside of his right arm is the number 9, his shirt number for both Spain and Atletico. On the inside of his left arm is his name, Fernando written in Tengwar, the script invented by J.R.R. Tolkien in *The Lord of the Rings*. The third is on his left shin and features the Roman numerals VII VII MMI (7 7 2001), to mark the date of his first kiss with girlfriend Olalla.

— LET THERE BE LIGHT —

In the autumn of 1957, Liverpool played Everton at Goodison Park to commemorate the 75th anniversary of the Liverpool County FA. Everton won 2–0 but the stranger aspect of the match was it was the first time a game had been played at Goodison under floodlights.

Not to be outdone, the Liverpool board installed pylons at each corner of Anfield and it was Everton who came to play the first match under the new £12,000 lights. Liverpool won 3–2. Those pylons remained until March 1973 when the new Main Stand was built and included a new lighting system that spread along the roof of the new stand and the opposite Kemlyn Road Stand at a cost of £100,000.

— GOD IS A KOPITE (NO ROBBIE, THE OTHER ONE) —

In July 1984, American preacher and personal friend of God himself Billy Graham (according to Woody Allen the two go on double dates together) came to England to spread the word. Graham toured the country to sell-out crowds and spent seven nights sermonising at Anfield in front of a full Kop end. With that in mind, it's worth remembering two bits of graffiti reportedly seen near Anfield in years gone by:

Poster on Wall: WHAT WOULD YOU DO IF JESUS CHRIST CAME TO LIVERPOOL?
Graffiti: MOVE IAN ST JOHN TO INSIDE LEFT

Message on wall: JESUS SAVES . . .
Graffiti: . . . BUT KEEGAN SCORES ON THE REBOUND

— WE'LL HAVE TO CALL IT OFF —

At the beginning of the 2006/07 season Liverpool arranged a reserve game against AC Milan's second string side. It was penciled in for the end of the campaign in Italy on May 23rd 2007. Unfortunately, the game had to be called off. The two clubs instead were meeting in Athens that night in the small matter of a Champions League final.

— PAISLEY'S PROVERBS —

"If you're in the penalty area and don't know what to do with the ball, put it in the net and we'll discuss the options later."
Bob Paisley

"Mind you, I've been here during the bad times too – one year we came second."
Bob Paisley

"I'll tell you something, they shot the wrong f*****g Kennedy!"
Bob Paisley to Alan Kennedy after a bad first half in his debut as a Liverpool player

"The sort of lad I'm looking for here is a kid who'll try to nutmeg Kevin Keegan in a training match . . . but then step aside for him in the corridor."
Bob Paisley on his ideal young pro

"He's not very fast but he is nippy."
Bob Paisley on the merits of an opponent

"If you have all had enough of winning then come and see me and I'll sell the lot of you."
Bob Paisley

"I'm surprised they don't charge me rent and rates."
Bob Paisley on his eleventh trip to Wembley

"We'd better get out of Glasgow before they realise what they've done."
Bob Paisley after signing Kenny Dalglish from Celtic for £440,000

— HANDBAGS AT 3PM —

During the 1963/64 season, Everton goalkeeper Gordon West made the mistake of blowing a kiss to his barrackers on the Kop. The following September when he returned to the Kop end, the fans had a present for him. A handbag. A handbag with his name painted across it. On this occasion though, the Evertonian had the last laugh. The Blues won 4–0.

— YOU TOOK YOUR TIME, LAD —

When in the 19th minute of a match on December 3rd 2005, Peter Crouch bundled the ball past Mike Pollitt in Wigan Athletic's goal, he finally broke a run of 18 games without a goal for his new club. The 1,228 minutes it took Crouchy to net for the Reds is a record among Liverpool's post-war strikers who went on to play more than ten games for the club. The big man shouldn't feel too embarrassed, however, as he's among exulted company. Even Rushie was in no hurry to get started and no one has scored more. Here are the top ten post-war goalscoring ditherers:

Player	Games	Minutes
Peter Crouch	18	1,228
Arthur Rowley	11	Didn't score in 11 games for the club
Ian Rush	10	813
Michael Robinson	10	784
Jack Balmer	6	531
Kevin Baron	6	527
Phil Boersma	7	480
Emile Heskey	5	436
Les Shannon	5	382
Alf Arrowsmith	5	361

— ANYONE FOR TENNIS? —

You may think that the closest tennis has come to Anfield was when Vinnie Jones and John Fashanu were running amok in the name of Wimbledon FC. You would be wrong.

During the 1920s and 1930s white flannels and strings replaced red shirts and studs. In the summer months, boards would be laid on the hallowed turf, nets would be put in place and umpires would take to their seats. This was no lower league stuff either. Spectators would come to the Kop to see the likes of American star and world number one 'Big' Bill Tilden, and England's three time Wimbledon champ Fred Perry. Whether the Kopites enjoyed Pimms and strawberries with their tennis is not documented.

— MOST CONSECUTIVE GAMES —

Having missed an uncomfortable European Cup trip to Trabzonspor of Turkey in the autumn of 1976, Phil Neal was back in the side for the next match on October 23rd. The game (a 1–1 draw at Leeds) was the first of 417 consecutive games the marauding right back played for Liverpool.

Neal didn't miss a game for nearly seven years before sitting out a First Division fixture at home to Sunderland on October 1st 1983, which the Wearsiders won 1–0. He was back in the side the following week. Here's the top ten longest runs of games by Liverpool players:

Player	No. of games	From	To
Phil Neal	417	Oct 23rd 1976	Sep 24th 1983
Ray Clemence	336	Sep 9th 1972	Mar 4th 1978
Bruce Grobbelaar	317	Aug 29th 1981	Aug 16th1986
Chris Lawler	316	Oct 2nd 1965	Apr 24th 1971
David James	213	Feb 19th 1994	Feb 23rd 1998
Alan Kennedy	205	Jan 23rd 1982	Mar 31st 1985
Ian Callaghan	185	Aug 17th 1971	Sep 7th 1974
Kenny Dalglish	180	Aug 13th 1977	Aug 23rd 1980
Emlyn Hughes	177	Oct 31st 1972	Oct 25th 1975
Peter Thompson	153	Sep 1st 1965	Apr 13th 1968

— BEGINNERS LUCK, MY ARSE! —

When Pepe Reina, on a bright May afternoon, dived to his right and saved Anton Ferdinand's penalty in Cardiff, not only had he ensured his club their seventh FA Cup victory but the agile keeper also guaranteed his manager and compatriot a little slice of Liverpool history. With the 2006 FA Cup won and the 2005 Champions League still a wonderfully vivid memory, Rafa Benitez became the first manager in Liverpool's history to win two major trophies in each of his first two seasons.

Ok, so John McKenna, Liverpool's inaugural boss won the Lancashire League and the Second Division titles in 1893 and 1894 but you get the drift. It took Bill Shankly three seasons to win promotion and it took Bob Paisley a trophy-less 1974/75 season to exorcise the ghost of his mercurial predecessor. Joe Fagan's 1983/84 treble was followed up with a barren season, Kenny Dalglish couldn't match his 1985/86 double in his second term, Souness' only trophy came in his first season as did Roy Evans', whilst Gerard Houllier took two seasons to bring in the silverware.

— RED LEGENDS: IAN RUSH —

Liverpool's record goalscorer

Was there ever a better bit of advice given at Anfield? Was there ever a more productive pep talk? In 1981, Ian Rush, Liverpool's new young centre-forward was struggling; struggling for confidence and struggling for goals. His manager Bob Paisley took him to one side. "You have to be more selfish," he told him, adding that Rush was going on the transfer list. He wasn't, of course, but the manager's words had the desired effect.

In September that year, Finnish champions Oulu Palloseura were the visitors to Anfield. Rush was on the bench, a spot the youngster feared would be as good as it got for him at Liverpool. Paisley's men were cruising and in the second-half he sent Rush on for David Johnson. Four minutes later and at last he had got a goal. It may have simply made the score 5–0 but to Rush it meant everything. He could score goals and he went on to notch another 345 for the club, more than any other man in history.

Ian Rush. The very name screams goals. In his first spell at the club before leaving for a year at Juventus in 1987, Rush couldn't stop scoring. His ability to time a run, his incredible turn of pace, and deadly finishing made him the perfect striker. His goals won four titles, four League Cups in a row, an FA Cup and, in 1984, the European Cup. That 1983/84 season was Rush's finest. His 47 goals made him a European star. Napoli tried to sign him before turning their interests to one Diego Maradona, and so Italy would have to wait. Before his move to Juventus, Rush helped Liverpool to the Double in 1986 and in his last season scored another 30 league goals. Fans started a campaign to keep him at the club but to no avail.

Kenny Dalglish built a new, improved team to appease those fans but when, in the summer of 1988, it became clear that Rush could come home, the Liverpool boss snapped him up for a record £2.8m. Rush wouldn't have things all his own way in his first season back, though. John Aldridge and Peter Beardsley were too good to stand back and let him back in, but he bided his time, came on as a substitute against Everton in the FA Cup final and scored two goals to win the match.

Rush's second spell at the club was maybe not as prolific in terms of goalscoring, but he had matured into a fine all-round player. He was the perfect, wiser foil for the young Robbie Fowler and as captain he lifted the 1995 League Cup at Wembley. In 1996 he bade farewell to the club once more, this time for good, with the goalscoring records set in stone and in no danger of being overturned. It was BBC sports legend David Coleman who once said that "Goals pay the rent", if that is the case, Rush paid off his mortgage years ago.

Ian Rush fact-file

Appearances	658
Goals	346
Wales caps while at Liverpool	67

Honours	**Seasons**
First Division Championship	1981/82
	1982/83
	1983/84
	1985/86
	1989/90
FA Cup	1986
	1989
	1992
League Cup	1980/81
	1981/82

	1982/83
	1983/84
	1994/95
European Cup	1983/84
Charity Shield	1982
	1986*
	1989
	1990*
Football Writers' Player of the Year	1984
PFA Player of the Year	1984
PFA Young Player of the Year	1983

*Shared

— YOU LEFT YOUR POPCORN, ALBERT? —

In September 1946, Newcastle United's centre-forward Albert Stubbins sat in a Geordie cinema ready to watch an early evening motion picture. As he got comfortable, a notice flashed on to the screen. "Would Albert Stubbins please report to St James' Park." Both Liverpool and Everton were looking to sign the striker and it was time to make a decision (see *Heads or Tails*, page 73).

— SGT PEPPER TAUGHT THE REDS TO PLAY —

On June 1st 1967 the second best thing to come out of Liverpool released their eighth album. *Sgt Pepper's Lonely Hearts Club Band* by The Beatles was an immediate success for the Fab Four both with the critics and the punters. The music remains as popular today of course, but it is the iconic album cover that immediately comes to mind when *Sgt Pepper* is brought up, and in that world famous image is a little bit of Liverpool Football Club.

The cover, designed by Peter Blake, features – as well as the band – cardboard cut-outs of numerous famous faces from Marlon Brando to Oscar Wilde and W.C. Fields to Karl Marx. But look closer and there, just to the right of George Harrison, just behind Marlene Dietrich, is Liverpool centre-forward from 1946 to 1952 and scorer of 82 goals, Albert Stubbins. It was writer and The Beatles biographer, Hunter Davies who convinced the guys that they should have a Merseyside footballer on their new cover.

LIVERPOOL

Home and Away Kits
1892-2010

www.historicalkits.co.uk

1892-94

1947-48

1900-01 (change)

1900-02

1903-04

1905-07

1907-10

1910-31

1928-29 (change)

1931-32

1932-33

1934-35

1935-36

1936-40

1944-45

1946-50 (change)

1947-49

1949-51

1950 (FA Cup Final)

1951-55

1955-59

1957-58 (change)

1959-62

1960-61 (change)

1962-63

1963-64

1964-69

1964-69 (change)

1969-70 (change)

1969-76

1972-73 (change)

1974 (FA Cup Final)

1976-78 (change)

1976-79

1976-79 (third)

1977 (FA Cup Final)

1978-79 (change)

1979-81 (third)

1979-82

1979-82 (change)   1981-82 (third)   1982-83

1982-84 (change)   1983-85   1984-85 (change)

1985-86   1985-86 (change)   1985-86 (third)

1986-87   1986-87 (change)   1986-87 (third)

1986 (FA Cup Final)   **1987-88**   **1987-88 (change)**

1988 (FA Cup Final)   **1988-89**   **1988-89 (change)**

1988-89 (third)   **1989-91**   **1989-1991 (change)**

1989 (FA Cup Final)   **1991-92**   **1991-92 (change)**

1992-93　　　　1992-93 (change)　　　1992 (FA Cup Final)

1993-95　　　　1993-95 (change)　　　1994-96 (third)

1995-96　　　　1995-96 (change)　　　1996 (FA Cup Final)

1996-98　　　　1996-97 (change)　　　1997-98 (change)

1998-2000

1998-99 (change)

1999-2000 (change)

2000-02

2000-01 (change)

2001 (FA Cup Final)

2001-02 (change)

2001-03 (Europe)

2002-04

2002-03 (change)

2003-04 (change)

2004-05 (change)

2004-06

2005-06 (change)

2005-06 (Europe)

2006-08

2006-07 (change)

2006-07 (third)

2007-08 (change)

2007-08 (third)

2008-09

2008-09 (change)

2008-09 (third)

2009-10 (change)

— HEADS OR TAILS? —

Over the years many factors have been attributed to Liverpool's fantastic success. Honest, hard work; simple training methods, the best in management and, of course, the finest players around. Another major factor though mustn't be ignored. Good, old fashioned luck! On two occasions Liverpool have relied on literally the toss of a coin, and on both occasions they finished with smiles on their faces:

- In 1946 prolific centre-forward Albert Stubbins arrived back at St James' Park with a decision to make (see *You Left Your Popcorn Albert*, page 72). His 244 goals for Newcastle had attracted a number of clubs and Liverpool's manager George Kay had made the trip to try and convince him that his future lay at Anfield. Hot on his heels on the road from Merseyside was Everton boss Theo Kelly who was also in Toon with high hopes of signing the copper-topped goal getter.

  Stubbins wondered who to talk to first, who could set their stall out and impress him before their rival? Stubbins was a fair man so he tossed a coin and it fell in Kay's favour. He talked first and due to a great sell Stubbins' mind was immediately made up. Kelly and Everton didn't get a look in and Liverpool got their man, Stubbins got his goals, and thanks to all 24 of them, Liverpool won the League Championship that season.

- After 330 minutes of gruelling European Cup football (home and away matches and a play-off at neutral ground), Liverpool and FC Koln (Cologne) still couldn't be separated. After two 0–0 draws the teams had drawn 2–2 in the Rotterdam play-off. This was 1965, the torture of penalties was yet to be introduced, and so a coin (actually it was a coloured disc) would have to be used to decide the winner of this quarter-final.

  Ron Yeats, Liverpool's captain, stepped up as the referee prepared to toss the disc, red on one side, white on the other – the colours of the two teams. If it landed red side up, Liverpool would be through to their first European Cup semi-final. White and they would be out. The referee tossed the disc into the air, but amazingly it came down and stuck straight up in the mud. It would have to be thrown again. Up it went once more, span a few times and landed with players huddling around to see the outcome. Up went Yeats' arms. It was red and Liverpool were through.

— DIEGO IS GOBSMACKED —

Anyone who had witnessed the incredible events unfold in Istanbul on May 25th 2005 couldn't help but have an opinion. Diego Maradona, like everyone else, couldn't quite believe what he had just seen. "Even the Brazil team that won the 1970 World Cup could not have staged a comeback with Milan leading 3–0," he suggested. "Liverpool showed that miracles exist. After this game, my English team is going to be Liverpool."

— OUTFOXED —

There are bogey teams and there is Leicester City. What is it with the Foxes? Even in Liverpool's pomp, the Reds would take on and beat the finest that Europe had to offer; put them up however against the men from Filbert Street and usually they crumbled.

Leicester ended Liverpool's 85 game unbeaten run at Anfield between 1978 and 1981, but their hoodoo over the Reds goes back further. Back in 1963, a Gordon Banks inspired City denied Liverpool an FA Cup final place, winning their semi-final 1–0 at Hillsbrough, and in fact in each of Liverpool's first three seasons back in the First Division in the early 1960s, Leicester came to Anfield and won.

Liverpool and Leicester were invited to play the 1971 Charity Shield (Double winners Arsenal were too busy apparently) and of course it was Leicester who won 1–0. Bill Shankly's last championship-winning team in 1972/73 came unstuck against the Foxes, too, losing 3–2 at their place. And it doesn't stop there.

During the 1980s Leicester beat Liverpool four times. In the 1983/84 treble season, the Reds failed to beat the pesky Foxes; the following season Leicester won at Anfield and the start of the 1986/87 campaign saw Leicester beat the champions 2–1 at Filbert Street. There's more.

Promoted back into the Premiership in 1996, Leicester won at Anfield in August 1997, did the double over Liverpool in the 1998/99 season before winning at Anfield once more at the end of the 1999/00 efforts, a result that cost the Reds Champions League football.

Foxes. A damn nuisance if you ask me.

— IAN RUSH: INDIE BAND —

You'll know and love him as Liverpool's all-time top goalscorer, but Ian Rush is also the name of an Indie band from Wales. Want to know more? Go to www.ian-rush.co.uk.

— GRAZIE IL DUCE —

May 20th 1931 and Scotland are playing Italy in Rome. Scotland's esteemed captain is also Liverpool's left-half Jimmy McDougall, who prior to the game is presented with a bouquet of flowers from none other than Benito Mussolini. McDougall therefore is, as far as we know, the only Liverpool player to ever receive flowers from a Fascist dictator and tyrant.

— HE LEAPT LIKE A KIPPE —

Liverpool's little known Norwegian defender Frode Kippe boasted a strange sporting hobby. Players have always admitted to a penchant for golf, snooker or fishing. Not Kippe. A bit-part member of the 2001 treble squad, he used to be a more than useful ski jumper.

Kippe, aged 16 was actually his country's ski jump youth champion. Norway's biggest hill is called Holmenkollen. The record jump ever recorded off of it is 126 meters. Kippe in his teens managed a very respectable 105m. Unfortunately he could never make the same leap into the Liverpool first team and made only two appearances before leaving in 2002.

— JOB DONE —

Bob Paisley's last season was a memorable one. He climbed the Wembley steps to pick up the League Cup, and he watched all season as his team, inspired by a strike force of Ian Rush and Kenny Dalglish, tore First Division defences apart. So strong were his 1982/83 League Championship winners that they were confirmed as champions with seven games still to play.

With the trophy won, cue a collapse of English cricket-like proportions. From those last seven games, Liverpool won just two points and actually lost Paisley's last ever league game in charge at second placed Watford. Despite Liverpool's sloppy finish to the season, Graham Taylor's side still finished 11 points behind Paisley's men.

— THE WORLD CUP HUNT —

Of the Liverpool men who have played in a World Cup, only Roger Hunt has played on the winning side in the final – for England in 1966. The only other player to get close was German midfielder Dietmar Hamann who reached the final in 2002 but lost 2–0 to Brazil in Tokyo.

— WHAT'S ON YOUR IPOD? —

Before the 2007 European Cup final in Athens a selection of Liverpool players were asked what they would be listening to, to get geed up for the job at hand. Here are the (sometimes dodgy) results. Yes that means you Agger!:

Player	Song
Peter Crouch	'The Weekend (Come and Get up Everybody)' – Byron Stingley
Steven Gerrard	'Dakota' – Stereophonics
Jamie Carragher	'Waterfall' – The Stone Roses
Jamie Carragher	'In My Life'– Johnny Cash
Pepe Reina	'The Training Montage from *Rocky IV*'
Pepe Reina	'Eye of the Tiger' – Survivor
Robbie Fowler	'Everybody's Changing' – Keane
Luis Garcia	'Say it Right' –Nelly Furtado
Sami Hyypia	'Numb/Encore' – Jay Z and Linkin Park
Craig Bellamy	'Red Red Wine' – UB40
Xabi Alonso	'Stand by Me' – Oasis
Daniel Agger	'Gardens Tale' – Volbeat (Danish heavy metal!)
Whole Squad	'Ring of Fire' – Johnny Cash
Whole Squad	'You'll Never Walk Alone' – Gerry and the Pacemakers

— WHAT'S WITH THE WHITE PATCHES? —

Take a look at the old pictures of Liverpool's third European Cup triumph against Real Madrid in 1981 and you will notice that on the players' shirts, where the kit manufacturer's logo should be, is a white patch. This is because Umbro, Liverpool's then kit supplier, hadn't put any cash into the Uefa kitty and so it was adjudged that their logo should not be allowed to be advertised in the Paris final.

The English-based firm though needn't have worried too much. Plenty of the Liverpool players knew once they had won that they would get a few extra quid for being seen with the logo, so come the final whistle the sticker came off.

— HE WON IT FOUR TIMES, HE WON IT FOUR TIMES —

When Liverpool beat Rome in their own back yard to win a fourth European Cup in 1984, Phil Neal was the only player to have played in each of that glorious quartet. Messrs Gerrard and Carragher still need one more if they are to enter the club of Liverpool's multiple European trophy winners. Here is that club*:

Player	Medals	Years won
Phil Neal	4	1977, 1978, 1981, 1984
Jimmy Case	3	1977, 1978, 1981
Ray Clemence	3	1977, 1978, 1981
Kenny Dalglish	3	1978, 1981, 1984
Alan Hansen	3	1978, 1981, 1984
Ray Kennedy	3	1977, 1978, 1981
Terry McDermott	3	1977, 1978, 1981
Graeme Souness	3	1978, 1981, 1984
Steve Heighway	2	1977, 1978
Alan Kennedy	2	1981, 1984
Sammy Lee	2	1981, 1984
Phil Thompson	2	1978, 1981

*This list includes players who played (either from the start or as a sub) in winning finals

— EL CHIP OFF THE OLD KOP —

Liverpool's two Spaniards in the 2007 European Cup Final, Xabi Alonso and Pepe Reina, both followed their fathers into professional football. Xabi's dad Miguel (known as Periko) played for Real Sociedad, Barcelona and Spain. When Pepe Reina walked out onto the field in Athens, however, he was following directly in the footsteps of his father, also called Miguel.

Reina Senior was a goalkeeper for Atletico Madrid who in 1974 reached the European Cup final in Brussels where they faced Franz Beckenbauer's Bayern Munich. The final itself finished 1–1 and with the absence of penalties (no chance to see the Reina penalty saving gene at work then) it went to a replay which the Germans won 4–0.

— GREAT GAFFERS: KENNY DALGLISH —

Not only did Kenny Dalglish have to deal with being the club's first ever player-manager, he also had to set about re-establishing morale in the club after the awful events of Heysel. As ever, Dalglish did it all with tenacity and consummate skill.

The start of his first season in charge was solid enough, but Manchester United looked like running away with the league after winning their first ten games. On November 26th 1985, United came to Anfield for a League Cup tie and were defeated thanks to two Jan Molby goals (the first an absolute belter), a setback which seemed to derail their whole season. Molby was becoming a hero and Dalglish appeared to have got to grips with his new role.

He wasn't playing much, though, and come February 1986, the side looked well off the pace. Dalglish decided to get his boots back on and helped Liverpool go on a run that took them to the brink of a 16th title. On the final day, Liverpool needed to win at Chelsea (never the happiest of stomping grounds) to take the title ahead of city rivals and reigning champs Everton. Chelsea chairman Ken Bates told anyone who would listen before the game that "Liverpool will win the championship over my dead body," but it was the Reds' boss who dug Bates' metaphorical grave with a fine volleyed goal that won the match.

A week later, the Double was won for the first time with victory over Everton in the FA Cup final. Dalglish was making this managerial lark look easy. It wasn't, of course, but Dalglish was now becoming more boss than player-boss and set about building a new, improved team without Ian Rush.

The side that took the title in 1987/88 is among the best ever seen at Anfield with John Barnes, Peter Beardsley and John Aldridge the stand-out forwards in a brilliant line-up. Another Double looked on but a cup final defeat to Wimbledon put paid to those dreams.

Ian Rush's return saw Dalglish's team push hard once more for honours the following season but 1988/89 will always be remembered for the events at Hillsborough. Liverpool won the cup that season and were pipped to the title by Arsenal but football mattered little and you could see the spark had been drained from Dalglish by yet another disaster.

The next season he got on with things and the title was won in 1989/90 but halfway through the following year he shocked the world of football by resigning. Dalglish had given so much, but now his health was suffering and it was time to stop. He eventually returned to management with Blackburn, taking the Lancashire side to the Premiership title and silencing those critics who suggested his successes with Liverpool had come too easily. That, though, was 'King Kenny's' way – he just made things look easy.

Kenny Dalglish fact-file

Games in charge	307

Honours	Season
First Division Championship	1985/86
FA Cup	1986
First Division Championship	1987/88
FA Cup	1989
First Division Championship	1989/90

— SUPERSUBS —

Ian Rush did it in the 1989 FA Cup Final, Vladimir Smicer did it in Istanbul in 2005. Ever since Geoff Strong came of the bench for the first time in 1965 and scored a goal, Liverpool substitutes have made a habit of changing games.

No one, however, has done it more famously or more times than David 'Supersub' Fairclough. It was he (also known affectionately on the Kop, due to his orange hair, as 'the Bionic Carrot') who came on against St Etienne in the closing stages of the 1977 European Cup quarter-final and scored the vital goal that sent the club on their way to European glory (see *A Night Like No Other*, page 13). Fairclough may not have liked the label, but the records show that he was indeed the club's all-time 'Supersub'.

Here are Liverpool's top five scorers from the bench:

Player	Goals scored as Sub
David Fairclough	18
Djibril Cisse	7
Ian Rush	6
Vladimir Smicer	6
Michael Owen	6

— WHITE TOP = WHITE FLAG —

Each time Liverpool have won a European Cup final they have worn their home red shirt and the opponents have played in the same colour. All five losing sides; Borussia Monchengladbach, Bruges, Real Madrid, Roma (away) and AC Milan (away) wore white. Unfortunately this record did not extend to the 2007 final against AC Milan.

— CALLAGHAN'S THE MAN —

On April 16th 1960, Ian Callaghan, a local lad just turned 18, made his debut for Liverpool in a 4–0 win over Bristol Rovers at Anfield, a game after which he was applauded off by his impressed team-mates.

A pacy, skilful winger, Callaghan had caught the eye since joining as a 16-year-old. On retiring, the great Billy Liddell was asked who could possibly replace him. He confidently stated that there was a youngster in the ranks more than able. That youngster was Callaghan and 17 years after that debut he was still proving Liddell right and an integral part of the team that won Liverpool's first ever European Cup.

Callaghan had made the journey with the club from the Second Division to league and European Champions. Along the way he made an incredible 857 games for the club, a record that looks in no danger of being broken.

Here are Liverpool's top ten appearance makers:

Player	Seasons	Appearances
Ian Callaghan	1960–78	857
Ray Clemence	1967–81	665
Emlyn Hughes	1967–79	665
Ian Rush	1980–87 and 1988–96	660
Phil Neal	1974–85	650
Tommy Smith	1963–78	638
Bruce Grobbelaar	1981–94	628
Alan Hansen	1977–90	620
Jamie Carragher	1997–	577
Chris Lawler	1963–75	549

— WHERE DID YOU GET THAT SUIT? —

It's hard to know what was the worst thing about May 17th 1996. Watching Manchester United's Eric Cantona score a late winner and lift the FA Cup to go with the Premiership title they had won the week before was one thing, as was the knowledge that a talented young Liverpool team had woefully underachieved that afternoon. It was a bad day made worse by the choice of suit adopted by the Liverpool squad. Cup final suits can often be affronts to fashion but the cream Armani numbers worn by Roy Evans' team that afternoon were particularly bad.

— TIME TO RAISE THE ROOF LADS! —

By the late 1920s, Liverpool were one of the big names in English football. The Reds had won back-to-back titles in 1922 and 1923 and crowds at Anfield regularly topped 50,000. The Kop had by now become famous in its own right and in 1928 the club's owners decreed that to accommodate a growing army of fans the end should be extended and covered with a giant roof, making it by far the biggest and most impressive covered terrace in the country.

The new, improved and covered Kop measured 135ft from the back row to the front and reached 50ft in height. On August 25th 1928, before the opening game of the season against Bury, the impressive new structure was opened by 'Honest' John McKenna, previously a secretary, director and president of the club who was by now the president of the Football League.

Spectators were asked to be in their places 15 minutes before kick-off when McKenna strolled out onto the pitch and unfurled a commemorative flag in front of the Kop. After the game (which Liverpool won 3–0, taking only a minute to score their first goal in front of the covered fans), McKenna was presented with a gold cigar holder and gave a speech.

"Now that the spectators are assured of more comfortable conditions, I would like to give a word of advice to the directors to devote their finances, energy and intelligence to create a team worthy of the splendid surroundings."

— WHO'S A NAUGHTY BOY THEN? —

In the history of the club, no one has been sent off more times than the current captain Steve Gerrard. On five occasions Stevie G has been asked to take an early bath. Tut tut, Stevie lad.

Here are Gerrard's red cards:

Date	Opposition	Venue	Score
Sep 27th 1999	Everton	Anfield	0–1
Apr 13th 2001	Leeds	Anfield	1–2
Sep 8th 2001	Aston Villa	Anfield	1–3
May 11th 2003	Chelsea	Stamford Bridge	1–2
Mar 25th 2006	Everton	Anfield	3–1

— A DUTCH MASTER —

Liverpool fans have been lucky enough to cheer on some of the greatest players this country has ever seen – Liddell, Hunt, Keegan, Dalglish, Rush, Barnes and Gerrard; fantastic players to name a few. But of the opposition to have faced the Reds, one man stands out.

In the 1966/67 season Liverpool re-entered the European Cup hoping to go one better than the semi-final they reached in 1965. They struggled past Romanians, Petrolul Ploesti in the first round and so were drawn with the Dutch side Ajax, far from a known force in the European game at the time. In the Ajax side was a 19-year-old called Johann Cruyff, who although far from the world star he would soon become gave Bill Shankly's side an early indication of the talent that he possessed.

Liverpool travelled to the Netherlands for the first leg to be greeted by a thick Amsterdam fog. Shankly felt the game should be postponed but the officials were satisfied that it should go ahead. In awkward conditions, the only thing clear was that in Cruyff, Ajax possessed a world-beater and he set about the Liverpool defence, scoring one as the Dutch took a massive 4–0 first-half lead. At 2–0, Shankly had taken advantage of the conditions and strolled onto the pitch without the referee's knowledge to tell his men to hold out and get them back to Anfield. They couldn't and, despite a better second-half show, they lost 5–1.

This, though, was Bill Shankly and he some somehow managed to convince the Liverpool fans that the second leg would be an historic night and the deficit would be clawed back. Over 54,000 fans believed him and came to Anfield, only to bear witness to another master class in the art of passing and movement from the young Cruyff who scored twice in a 2–2 draw.

Liverpool got their revenge in 1976 when Cruyff, by now with Barcelona, were beaten in the semi-final of the Uefa Cup. It was in that same competition, in 2001, that Cruyff was once more beaten by Liverpool. This time it was his son, Jordi, who despite scoring a last gasp equaliser for Spanish side Alaves in the final, lost 5–4 to Gerard Houllier's men.

— LIVERPOOL'S OLDEST DEBUTANT —

At an age when most players have hung up their boots, bought a pub and expanded their waistlines, Ted Doig made his debut for Liverpool Football Club. On September 1st 1904, aged 37 years and 307 days Doig, the club's new goalkeeper, took to the field as Liverpool began their season at home to Burton United. Liverpool won 2–0 and won the Second Division title that season with Doig an ever-present.

— DAD'S RED ARMY —

Not content with dominating the English game as pro footballers, Liverpool's old boys have also won the UK Masters Cup more often than any other team. Since its inception in 2000, Liverpool have won the trophy twice, in 2001 and 2002. In 2006, Liverpool also won the Dubai Masters. The impressive squad that won the 2002 event was:

Player	Seasons at Liverpool
Bob Boulder	1983–1985
Alan Kennedy	1978–1985
Phil Neal	1974–1985
Ian Rush	1980–1987 and 1988–1996
Jan Molby	1984–1995
John Aldridge	1987–1989
Jimmy Case	1975–1981
John Durnin	1986–1989
Nigel Spackman	1987–1989
Paul Walsh	1984–1987

— FLY THE FLAG —

In the summer of 1928, at the same time that the Kop was extended and covered, Liverpool made one more addition to their ground. On the corner of the Kemlyn Road and Walton Breck Road, just inside the perimeter wall, a white flagpole was put in place. It wasn't any flagpole, mind. This one had originally been a mast on Isambard Kingdom Brunel's transatlantic steamer 'The Great Eastern', one of the first iron ships ever and at the time of her production the biggest ship in the word.

The Great Eastern made her maiden voyage in 1860 but 30 years later she had been broken up for scrap on the Mersey, to be used as an advertising hoarding for Lewis' department store and a funfair in the Liverpool Exhibition of 1887. The surviving topmast was later floated across the river and hauled up Everton Valley to Anfield by a team of horses. It is still at the ground. When the old Kop was demolished in 1994, the landmark was restored and remains at 'Flagpole Corner'.

— RED LEGENDS: ROBBIE FOWLER —

The scouse charm, the T-shirt in support of Liverpool's dockers, the cheeky goal celebrations, the four-fingered salute to Manchester United fans reminding them of how many European Cups Liverpool had won at the time, oh and the 183 goals in red. It's little wonder that Robbie Fowler is known as 'God' at Anfield.

Fowler burst on to the scene in the mid-nineties and with his impish talent, he immediately cleared away the clouds of what was becoming a gloomy fall from grace for Graeme Souness' team. The Scottish manager must be given credit for blooding Fowler, a young player who had shone for the England youth set-up and who had attracted a host of clubs before opting for Liverpool.

To be honest, Souness had little choice. In late 1993, his team were struggling for goals. Ian Rush was doing his bit but the likes of Paul Stewart and Nigel Clough were struggling. In a League Cup tie at Fulham, Souness gave youth it's chance and on an autumn night by the River Thames Reds fans had a new hero. He scored a great goal at Craven Cottage and he then followed that up with all five in the second leg at Anfield.

Souness wouldn't last long as manager but his successor, Roy Evans immediately built a side that would constantly create chances, and Fowler was always there to finish them off. He was Young Player of the Year in both 1995 and 1996 and also broke into the England squad.

Fowler provided many great memories. The quick hat-trick against Arsenal, the two goals at Old Trafford that upstaged Eric Cantona's return, the turn and shot at the Kop end against Aston Villa followed by a trademark slide head first into the net. Suddenly, Kopites had a player who they idolised with a fervour not seen since Kenny Dalglish's heyday. They even gave him the same chant as they afforded King Kenny.

An injury in 1997 curtailed Fowler's progress, as did the emergence of a new young goalscorer, Michael Owen. But however many goals Owen scored, however many games those goals won, he could never replace Fowler in the hearts of the fans. It wasn't Owen's fault, he just wasn't as raw as Fowler. Owen embodied the modern footballer, endorsed and sponsored, while Fowler was a throwback to another time.

Under Gerard Houllier, Fowler continued to score but he struggled to convince the Frenchman that he was the ideal partner for Owen. Emile Heskey was often preferred and despite a huge contribution to Liverpool's treble season, Fowler was sold to Leeds for £12m at the end of that year.

It was a blow. He moved on to Manchester City but you sensed his eyes were always on home, and in 2006, Rafa Benitez brought him back. The fans were delighted. Every Fowler goal was cheered with extra glee as if they knew the end was imminent. That end came in the spring of 2007. He said his farewells at Anfield after the last game of the season. A tear seemed to well in his eyes but he shouldn't worry. For as long as fans come to worship Liverpool, 'God' will always be in their thoughts.

Robbie Fowler fact-file

Appearances	369
Goals	183
England caps while at Liverpool	26

Honours	Season
FA Cup	2001
League Cup	2000/01
Uefa Cup	1994/95
2000/01	
Charity Shield	2001
PFA Young Player of the Year	1995
	1996

— SHOOT-OUT KINGS —

To date, Liverpool have been involved in 11 penalty shoot-outs, incredibly losing just once:

Penalty shoot-outs won

Year	Competition	Opponents	Score
1974	Charity Shield	Leeds	6–5
1984	European Cup final	AS Roma	4–2
1992	FA Cup semi-final	Portsmouth	3–1
1995	FA Cup third round	Birmingham	2–0
2001	League Cup final	Birmingham	5–4
2002	League Cup fourth round	Ipswich	5–4
2004	League Cup fifth round	Tottenham	4–3
2005	European Cup final	AC Milan	3–2
2006	FA Cup final	West Ham	3–1
2007	European Cup semi-final	Chelsea	4–1

Penalty shoot-outs lost

Year	Competition	Opponents	Score
1993	League Cup fourth round	Wimbledon	3–4

— WHERE'S OUR TROPHY? —

On April 18th 1964, Liverpool took on and beat Arsenal 5–0 to win their first League Championship title in 17 years. A crowd of 48,623 had crammed into Anfield (some queued all night to be sure of their attendance) and at the full-time whistle they celebrated with their usual fervour in anticipation of seeing the famous trophy. They would be disappointed.

It turned out that the Football League had failed to get the trophy to Anfield, and rumour has it that Everton – champions the previous season – had refused to hand the trophy over until the end of the season. Whatever the reason, the players and their ecstatic fans refused to be denied their party. While on the lap-of-honour, Liverpool captain Ron Yeats noticed that a young boy on the Kop had made a trophy out of papier-mâché and so went over and 'borrowed' the creation to ensure the players had something to show for their efforts.

— THE TRAINING GROUND —

The fans flock to see the action at Anfield but what they often don't see is the hard work that goes on behind the scenes on the training ground. That training ground is at Melwood.

Situated in the West Derby area of Liverpool, Melwood was bought by the club in 1950 from the neighbouring St Francis Xavier School. Prior to the purchase, Liverpool players used to train on a small bit of land that is now the Main Stand car park. Melwood back then was a simple place. Just a cold pavilion for the players to change in, and a few pitches. Like everything else at the club all that changed when Bill Shankly arrived in 1959.

Shankly, who lived around the corner, had a gym installed in 1961 and a new, improved pavilion in 1968. Target boards and five-a-side pitches were also brought in, while under the Scot the three-and-a-half mile jog from Melwood to Anfield was outlawed.

"We never bothered with sand dunes and hills and roads," Shankly later said. "We trained on grass where football is played."

So successful were the techniques devised by Shankly that little changed under Bob Paisley, Joe Fagan and Kenny Dalglish. It was Graeme Souness who arrived in 1991 who set about revamping Melwood, bringing in modern facilities such as baths! Today, Melwood is a state-of-the-art training facility and Rafa Benitez's men enjoy the best in pitches, swimming pools, gymnasiums and rehabilitation. Benitez has even had beds put in to ensure his men get their beauty sleep.

— WE TAUGHT HIM ALL HE KNEW —

Sir Matt Busby. Manchester United legend. The man who put United on the world map, the man who gave the fans the Busby Babes, the man who lauded over the golden era of Charlton, Law and Best. A legend so strong, even the usually unmovable Alex Ferguson bowed to his expertise. It could, though, have been oh so different, for Sir Matt actually played a massive part of his career at Liverpool and could easily have taken a job behind the scenes at Anfield.

In fact, the two English clubs Matt Busby played for were (and whisper this around Old Trafford) Manchester City and Liverpool! Having starred at Maine Road in the early 1930s as a creative half-back, Busby joined Liverpool in 1936 and immediately settled at the club and in the city where, according to a biography, he "rediscovered the simple joy of playing the game."

Busby had plenty of time for Liverpool boss George Kay, the feeling was mutual and Kay soon made him captain. He formed a great bond with the fans at Anfield and was at the peak of his form when the Second World War broke out. Then, after the war, came the crunch. With George Kay well settled in the manager's office, Liverpool, despite being very keen on Busby's obvious expertise, could only offer the Scot a coaching role at the club. Busby, though, was ambitious and wanted to manage a team in his own right and soon an opening came up at some other club along the East Lancs Road.

Such, though, was the esteem that Busby was held in at Anfield that in 1966 the fans were asked in a poll to name the club's greatest captain, a man to lead the club's all-time XI. That man was Matt Busby.

Matt Busby's record at Liverpool:

Signed from	Fee	Debut	Appearances	Goals
Manchester City	£8,000	Mar 14th 1936	125	3

— SKY TV'S FIRST EVER GOAL —

The first live Premiership match on Sky TV was between Nottingham Forest and Liverpool at the City Ground on August 16th 1992. The first (and only) goal of the match came after 29 minutes, courtesy of Teddy Sheringham, who curled a shot from 20-yards past David James in Liverpool's goal.

— CARRA'S EURO RECORD —

On Tuesday May 1st 2007, not only did the rock-like Jamie Carragher put in a brilliant performance against Chelsea in the ultimately victorious Champions League semi-final at Anfield but he also broke Ian Callaghan's record for European performances. Having made his European debut against Celtic on September 30th 1998, the second leg against Jose Mourinho's men was Carragher's 90th game in continental competition.

Here are Liverpool's top ten European performance makers (as of the end of the 2008/09 season):

Player	Seasons	Appearances
Jamie Carragher	1997–	116
Steven Gerrard	1998–	101
Sami Hyypia	1999–2009	94
Ian Callaghan	1960–1978	89
Tommy Smith	1963–1978	85
Ray Clemence	1967–1981	80
Emlyn Hughes	1967–1979	79
John Arne Riise	2001–2008	79
Phil Neal	1974–1985	74
Steve Heighway	1970–1981	67

— THE PAISLEY GATEWAY —

On April 8th 1999, the Paisley Gateway was opened to commemorate the monumental efforts of Liverpool's most successful manager.

Erected at the Kop End, the gates stand at an imposing four and half metres and weigh two tons. Their design includes the three European Cups Paisley won for the club, the crest of his birthplace in Hetton-le-Hole and that of Liverpool FC. On one of the brick pillars that flank the gates there is a picture of Paisley himself, on the other is a list of the many honours he brought to the club.

"If this was an Oscar ceremony I would be expected to fling my arms around, burst into tears and say Bob didn't deserve it," said Paisley's widow Jessie when officially opening the gates. "But though tears aren't far away, I'm not going to say that. If you ask me, if you ask me if Bob deserved it, I say yes, 100 per cent."

— ANFIELD'S GOALSCORING DEBUTANTS —

From Liverpool's first game at Anfield to the end of the 2006/07 season, 94 Liverpool players have scored on their debuts at Anfield. That first game, on September 3rd 1892, was an 8–0 win over Higher Walton and five players (Smith 2, McQue 2, Cameron 2, McBride, McVean) got on the scoresheet. Since then there have been plenty of notable examples of new boys introducing themselves to the fans in the best way possible, with a goal.

Here's a few of those first-timers:

Player	Date	Opposition	Score
Billy Liddell	Sep 7th 1946	Chelsea	7–4*
Roger Hunt	Sep 9th 1959	Scunthorpe	2–0
David Hickson	Nov 7th 1959	Aston Villa	2–1*
Bobby Graham	Sep 26th 1964	Aston Villa	5–1**
Kevin Keegan	Aug 14th 1971	Notts Forest	3–1
Kenny Dalglish	Aug 23rd 1977	Newcastle	2–0
John Aldridge	Feb 28th 1987	Southampton	1–0
John Barnes	Sep 12th 1987	Oxford United	2–0
David Speedie	Feb 9th 1991	Everton	3–1*
Stan Collymore	Aug 19th 1995	Sheffield Weds	1–0
Luis Garcia	Sep 11th 2004	WBA	3–0

* scored two
** scored three

— CHRIS REA PUTS THE FEAR OF GOD UP THE ROMANS —

Having taken an intimidating stroll around the Rome pitch before the 1984 European Cup final, the Liverpool players made their way back toward the dressing-rooms. 65,000 raucous Romans had let their feelings toward their visitors be known but, led by the always dogged Graeme Souness, the team had walked right in front of the their tormentors, proving they would not be unsettled.

As they approached the dressing-room in single file, David Hodgson, Craig Johnston and Souness began singing Chris Rea's 'I Don't Know What It Is, But I Love It'. Soon every player had joined in and as Roma manager, Nils Liedholm started to give his team-talk all could be heard was their opposition – supposedly in fear of what was essentially a home crowd – singing away outside their door.

— BIZARRE NAMES —

A number of Liverpool players have sported strange names. Here's a selection:

Player	Signed
Messina Allman	1934
Augustus Beeby	1908
Ernie Blenkinsop	1934
Reginald Blore	1959
Titi Camara	1999
Ned Doig	1904
Adolf Hanson	1931
Raby Howell	1898
Ephraim Longworth	1910

The strangest name though was actually not Christian or a surname. It was a middle name. It belonged to Mark Walters, signed by Graeme Souness in 1991. For some reason, Walters' parents gave him a very strange sounding middle name. Mark Everton Walters. Odd or what?

— THE FIRST EVER DERBY —

While official records will tell you that the first encounter between Liverpool and Everton was in the Reds' first season in the top flight in 1894, the truth is that the two met each other 18 months prior to that match in the final of the Liverpool Senior Cup.

The match took place at Bootle Football Club on April 22nd 1893, just over a year after Everton's acrimonious departure from Anfield. It may have been a mere local affair but as the Football League club, there was tremendous pressure on Everton. The directors at Goodison were clearly feeling the strain and hastily arranged a friendly with Scottish side Renton, just so they could field a weakened side against Liverpool and use that as an excuse in the event of an Everton defeat.

Ten thousand fans flocked to the final to see a physical, tense game in which Liverpool took a deserved lead through Wylie on the half hour. The rest of the game was as frantic, and in the last minute Everton claimed a penalty but the referee waved away their protests. Such was the Blues' anger at the decision, that the Liverpool FA officials refused to present the trophy and received a written protest about the referee, Herbie Arthur's performance. This was rejected and Everton Football Club were issued a warning about their poor conduct and sportsmanship.

— THE FIRST OF MANY —

By the beginning of the 20th century, Liverpool had yo-yoed between the First and Second Divisions. The closest they had come to winning the title was second place in 1898/99. Two seasons later, however, they would go one better and take the first of their 18 titles.

Tom Watson had been appointed as manager in 1896 and slowly but surely he had built a side capable of the performances needed to take the championship. At the back, skipper and giant Scot Alex Raisbeck was the rock on which the team's success was founded, while Sam Raybould was the centre-forward whose 16 goals would fire the club to success.

A home defeat to Everton in January 1901 looked to have ruined any thoughts of the title and by mid-February the team lay in eighth place, nine points off leaders Nottingham Forest. Watson's men, however, then went on a run that saw them go unbeaten in their last 12 games. Sunderland were beaten at Roker Park but, nevertheless, the Wearsiders remained top. Watson's men clawed back the deficit and needed a draw in the final game of the season at West Bromwich Albion to win the championship for the first time.

Already relegated, the Baggies were dogged in their resistance but a John Walker goal won the game and the team returned back to Liverpool Central Station to be greeted by thousands of ecstatic fans. Raisbeck was held shoulder high while a band played 'The Conquering Hero'. Once freed to go, the players and the board took a horse-drawn carriage back to Anfield and placed the trophy in the cabinet. A spot that, over the years, it would become extremely familiar with.

— SPOT ON KEEPER —

The first Liverpool keeper to save a penalty kick was Peter Platt, who thwarted Blackburn's Bob Crompton on February 6th 1904 in an FA Cup tie at Ewood Park. Unfortunately, Platt's heroics couldn't prevent a 3–1 defeat.

Bruce Grobbelaar has saved more penalties for Liverpool than any other keeper. On eight occasions in open play (sorry Jerzey and Pepe, shoot-outs don't count here) Brucie stopped penalties going past him. That's three more than both Tommy Lawrence and Ray Clemence, who both saved five.

— OOPS! —

As John Arne Riise trudged from the Anfield turf, having scored an own goal to give Chelsea a lifeline in the 2008 Champions League semi-final, Koppites would have missed the despair in his eyes as their own faces were tightly in their own hands. Riise though is far from alone. Here are some more high-profile gaffes:

- Bizarrely the first five own goals scored by Liverpool players came against Sunderland in five separate games between 1897 and 1930. The first was scored by Thomas Cleghorn at Anfield on December 27th 1897. The Reds lost 2–0.

- Between 1961 and 1967 Liverpool scored four own goals. All were put away by big Ron Yeats.

- On April 3rd 1980 Liverpool played Aston Villa at Anfield. A win would secure a 12th championship for the Reds. Having gone 1–0 up, Liverpool's Israeli international defender Avi Cohen put the ball past Ray Clemence to bring Villa level. In the second-half, Cohen scored again – this time in the right goal – to put the Reds back in front. The game finished 3–1 and the trophy stayed at Anfield.

- In a Milk Cup semi-final second-leg at Anfield on March 5th 1986, Liverpool chose to give Queens Park Rangers a helping hand to Wembley, scoring two own goals through Ronnie Whelan and Gary Gillespie and ensuring a 3–2 aggregate defeat. It wasn't the first time Liverpool had scored two own goals in one game. In 1961 Dick White managed to score two in a league game at Middlesbrough.

- We can't talk about own goals without mentioning Djimi Traore's neat back-heel in the 2005 FA Cup third round tie at Burnley. Poise, balance, a high degree of skill, Djimi had it all in that one moment. No wonder he went on to pick up a Champions League winners medal just months later. Thanks for the memories Djimi.

- "We all dream of a team of Carraghers!" That may be the case but when Jamie scored an own goal against West Ham in the 2006 FA Cup final in Cardiff he claimed the dubious honour of becoming the player who has scored the highest number of own goals in the club's history. It was his fifth, a total which included two in 1999 at the Kop end against Manchester United. Don't worry Jamie, we still love you.

— THE REAL MERSEYBEAT —

There is no official record of when singing on the terraces arrived in football. Going back to the game's roots in the late 19th century there are reports of fans breaking into song to cheer on their team, but Liverpool's Kop is generally considered to be the place where mass football singing began.

The summer of 1962 had seen a World Cup, held in Chile, beamed back to the television screens of Britain for the first time. During the final, Brazilian fans acclaimed their team by chanting "BRA-ZIL", clap, clap, clap; "BRA-ZIL", clap, clap, clap. It had a samba feel to it and during the opening game of the 1962/63 season against Blackpool, fervent Kopites immediately mimicked what they'd heard. "LIVER-POOL", clap, clap, clap, was soon ringing around the terrace.

Months later Beatlemania would grip the country and the Kop took this new-found expression of support one step further. Prior to games the Kop would sing along to the club's PA system playing that weeks top ten hits, invariably a Beatles tune and consequently a source of local pride.

Soon popular tunes like 'When The Saints Go Marching In' were adapted ("When The Reds . . ."), and when merseybeat band Gerry and the Pacemakers released 'You'll Never Walk Alone' in 1963, holding onto the number one spot for three weeks, it was immediately adopted by the Kop and the greatest football anthem of them all was sealed as the defining accompaniment to any significant Liverpool triumph, defeat or tragedy.

In 1964, with Beatlemania and the Merseybeat sweeping not only the country but the world; and with Bill Shankly's football team fast becoming a force in the English game, interest in all things Liverpool was rife. Couple that with the relatively new phenomenon that was the Kop and suddenly serious programmes such as *Panorama* were keen to take a closer look at the all-singing, all-swaying terrace behind Tommy Lawrence's goal.

"They don't behave like any other football fans," intoned the presenter. "Especially at one end of Liverpool's football ground, the Kop."

The show came to Anfield on April 18th 1964 to see Liverpool play Arsenal in a match that Shankly's men needed to win to clinch the title. The presenter could be seen standing in front of the Kop as the fans broke into renditions of a number of songs, including 'She Loves You' by The Beatles.

The presenter then said to camera:

"It used to be thought that that Welsh international rugby crowds were the most musical and passionate in the world, but I've never seen anything like this Liverpool crowd. On the field here, the gay and innovative ferocity they show is quite stunning. The Duke of Wellington before the battle of Waterloo said of his own troops, 'I don't know what they do to the enemy, but by god they frighten me.' I'm sure that some of the players in today's match must be feeling the same way."

Urged on by their noisy fans Liverpool beat Arsenal 5–0 to claim the title.

— ALUN'S TEENAGE ANGST —

In September 1968, Bill Shankly spent £110,000 on an 18-year-old striker from Wolves named Alun Evans; a transfer that made Evans British football's first ever six-figure teenager. Shankly, not usually so rash with his moves in the transfer market, had been extremely impressed with how Evans had given his 'Colossus' Ron Yeats the runaround in a recent encounter with the Molineux side and dived straight in. So impressed, in fact, was the Boss that instead of sticking Evans in the reserves he gave him an immediate debut against Leicester at Anfield on September 21st that year.

Evans scored in a 4–0 win and the following week got two in a 6–0 win over his old team Wolves. Sadly, though, his potential was never realised. He got a fine hat-trick in a Fairs Cup game against Bayern Munich in 1972, having picked up an FA Cup runners-up medal the season before, but having undergone surgery on his cartilage and witnessed the emergence of another youngster called Kevin Keegan, Evans joined Aston Villa before spells in America and Australia where he now lives. Having retired, Evans now works as a fish market delivery driver.

— IF THE CAP FITS —

The far off island of Trinidad may be a world away from the Whiston streets on which Steven Gerard first kicked a football but it was on the Caribbean island that, on June 1st 2008, Liverpool's captain won his 67th cap for England and equalled Ian Rush's record as the club's most capped player.

— THE TON CLUB —

Sixteen players have scored 100 goals or more for the club in all competitions. They are:

Player	Number of goals
Ian Rush	346
Roger Hunt	286
Gordon Hodgson	241
Billy Liddell	228
Robbie Fowler	176
Kenny Dalglish	172
Michael Owen	158
Harry Chambers	151
Jack Parkinson	130
Sam Raybould	128
Dick Forshaw	124
Steven Gerrard	120
Ian St John	118
Jack Balmer	111
John Barnes	108
Kevin Keegan	100

— THE WORST AUDITION EVER? —

On January 7th 1905, Chesterfield came to Anfield for a Division Two match fearing the worst. Liverpool were on fire having won all but one of their home games that season, scoring 25 goals along the way. Chesterfield's keeper was a Sam Hardy and it was he who had the misfortune that afternoon to collect the ball from his net on six occasions as Liverpool won 6–1.

Hardy, though, must have done something right that day as, at the end of the season, Liverpool paid £500 for his services and he eventually replaced Ned Doig, who had kept goal for the Reds for eight seasons. Hardy went on to play 240 games for Liverpool and 21 times for England.

— ZZ TOP —

In 115 years, Liverpool have had just two players whose surname begins with the letter Z. They are German Christian Ziege and Dutch midfielder Boudewijn Zenden.

— WERE YOU THERE? —

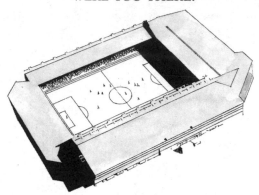

Liverpool's highest and lowest attendances:

Highest league attendance at Anfield: 58,757
v Chelsea, Division One, December 27th 1949 (2–2)

Highest FA Cup attendance at Anfield: 61, 905
v Wolverhampton Wanderers, fifth round, February 2nd 1952 (2–1)

Highest League Cup attendance at Anfield: 50,880
v Nottingham Forest, semi-final, second leg, February 12th 1980 (1–1)

Highest European attendance at Anfield: 55,104
v Barcelona, UEFA Cup semi-final, second leg, April 14th 1976 (1–1)

Lowest league attendance at Anfield: 1,000
v Loughborough , Division Two, December 7th 1895 (1–0)

Lowest post-war league attendance at Anfield: 11,976
v Scunthorpe, Division Two, April 22nd 1959 (3–0)

Lowest FA Cup attendance at Anfield: 4,000
v Newton, qualifying round, October 29th 1892 (9–0)

Lowest post-war FA Cup attendance at Anfield: 11,207
v Chester City , third round, second leg, January 9th 1946 (2–1)

Lowest League Cup attendance at Anfield: 9,902
v Brentford, second round second leg, October 25th 1983 (4–0)

Lowest European attendance at Anfield: 12,021
v Dundalk, European Cup first round, second leg, September 28th
1982 (1–0)

— MEET THE OWNERS 2:
GEORGE N. GILLETT JR —

- George N. Gillett Jr was born on October 22nd 1938 in Wisconsin.
- Gillett's first move into business came in 1970 when he started Gillett Communications and bought three television stations. He later branched out into newspapers.
- In 1985 Gillett acquired two ski resorts in Vail and Beaver Creek. Gillett was a huge supporter of alpine events and hosted the 1989 World Alpine Championships and the 1999 World Alpine Ski Championships. Today he owns resorts in New Hampshire, California, Washington and Wyoming.
- After financial difficulties in 1992, Gillett declared bankruptcy but remained on the payroll at the Vail Resort. In 1996 he had formed the Beaver Creek Ski Holdings Inc and bought his subsequent ski resorts.
- Gillett is also involved in food. His company deals with poultry, beef, lamb and sausages.
- Gillett's other business interests are in cars, landscaping and gardening products, and marine transportation.
- In 2000 Gillett paid $185m for 80 per cent of the Montreal Canadians, a hockey team in the NHL.
- Gillett has also had stakes in the Miami Dolphins and the Harlem Globetrotters basketball team.

— EPHRAIM REFRAINS FROM SCORING —

Ephraim Longworth was a consistent full back who played in the 1914 FA Cup final defeat against Burnley and won two First Division titles in 1922 and 1923. He also played five times for England. Longworth signed from Bolton in June 1910 and went on to play for 14 seasons, making 371 appearances (it would have been over 500 had it not been for the First World War) for the Reds, captaining the side on many occasions.

For all his loyal and sturdy service at right back, Longworth holds the dubious honour of the outfield player with the most appearances for the club without scoring a goal. In all of those 371 games, Ephraim failed to hit the target. Great defender though.

— PART OF THE FURNITURE —

For 21 years and 52 days, Elisha Scott was on Liverpool's books, making him the longest serving player in the club's history. Belfast-born, Scott's brother Billy had played in goal for Everton and recommended that the Toffees sign his younger sibling who had shown promise in the Ulster leagues. Everton thought the younger Scott *too* young but Liverpool chairman John McKenna quickly moved in and signed the 17-year-old in 1912.

On New Year's Day 1913, Scott made his first-team debut at home to Newcastle and kept a clean sheet, prompting the visiting team to make an offer to take the teenager with them when they left Anfield. The offer was turned down. The onset of the First World War disrupted Scott's progress and he had to wait until the start of the 1920/21 season until he was regarded as Liverpool's first choice keeper.

"He has the eye of an eagle, the swift movement of a panther when flinging himself at a shot and the clutch of a vice when gripping the ball," wrote one reporter as Scott became arguably the greatest keeper around. He won two league titles in 1922 and 1923 and became a firm favourite with the fans who stood behind him on the Kop.

In 1934 Everton made a cheeky bid for Scott. He was coming to the end of his career and the Liverpool board toyed with the idea of selling him, but a flood of protests in the local press persuaded them otherwise. On February 21st 1934, Scott played his 467th (a club record that stood until Billy Liddell broke it in 1957) and final game for the Reds in a 2–0 defeat at Chelsea.

At the end of that season, Scott stepped out into the directors' box to address the fans. Grown men shed tears as he said his goodbyes. Scott left to become player/manager of Belfast Celtic and died in 1959. Even today, he is regarded as one of the best goalkeepers that Liverpool have ever had.

— SORT IT OUT MARKUS —

Football players aren't renowned for their musical tastes but then again neither are Germans. Mix the two together and you're in trouble and so it is little surprise to learn that Markus Babbel, Liverpool's German full-back from 2000 to 2004, cites his favourite band as Krokus. Never heard of them? Don't bother putting them on your iPod unless of course you are into Swiss (very) heavy metal.

— MANY HAPPY RETURNS —

On October 7th 1922, Tom Bromilow scored for Liverpool in a rousing 5–1 win over Everton at Anfield. It was the perfect present for Bromilow who was also celebrating his 28th birthday that afternoon. Here's a selection of Reds who have scored for Liverpool on their birthdays:

Player	Date	Opposition	Result
Gordon Hodgson*	Apr 16th 1927	Bury	2–2
Robert Done	Apr 27th 1929	Blackburn	1–2
Adolf Hanson	Feb 27th 1937	Brentford	2–2
Berry Nieuwenhuys	Nov 5th 1938	Portsmouth	1–1
Billy Liddell	Jan 10th 1948	Nottingham Forest	4–1
John Evans	Aug 28th 1954	Derby	2–3
Jimmy Melia	Nov 1st 1958	Stoke	2–0
Steve Heighway	Nov 25th 1972	Tottenham	2–1
Phil Thompson	Jan 21st 1978	Birmingham	2–3
Terry McDermott	Dec 8th 1979	Aston Villa	3–1
Craig Johnston	Dec 8th 1981	Arsenal	3–0
Terry McDermott	Dec 8th 1981	Arsenal	3–0
Ronnie Whelan*	Sep 25th 1982	Southampton	5–0
Phil Neal	Feb 20th 1985	York	7–0
Steve McManaman	Feb 11th 1992	Bristol Rovers	2–1
David Burrows	Oct 25th 1992	Norwich	4–1
Robbie Fowler	Apr 9th 2006	Bolton	1–0
Peter Crouch	Jan 30th 2007	West Ham	2–1

*Scored twice

— WHAT'S ON THE MENU BOSS? —

In August 1974, just weeks after Bill Shankly had shocked the football world by announcing his retirement, his players organised a dinner for the man they would always call 'Boss'. This was a dinner for the players and their manager, the club had nothing to do with it and it was the players themselves who chipped in and paid for it. They had a menu made up with Shankly's image on it and food named in homage to the great man. As well as all the wine (strange as Shankly didn't drink) the players tucked into such delights as Clear Mersey Soup and Cured Kop Cod. Bon appétit . . .

— STEVIE'S EUROPEAN CUP MISSION —

When Steven Gerrard leapt to power in a header against PSV Eindhoven on April 3rd 2007, not only did it give Liverpool a vital lead in the Champions League quarter-final in Holland, it also made the Liverpool skipper the club's top scorer in Europe's premier club competition. It was his 15th effort and took him one beyond previous top scorer Ian Rush.

Here are Stevie's record 28 goals in the competition so far:

Date	Opposition	Goals	Final Score
Oct 16th 2001	Dynamo Kiev	1	2–1
Aug 10th 2004	Graz AK	2	0–2
Dec 8th 2004	Olympiakos	1	3–1
May 25th 2005	AC Milan	1	3–3
July 13th 2005	Total Network Solutions	3	3–0
July 19th 2005	Total Network Solutions	2	3–0
July 26th 2005	FBK Kaunas	1	3–1
Aug 2nd 2005	FBK Kaunas	1	2–0
Oct 31st 2006	Bordeaux	1	3–0
Nov 22nd 2006	PSV Eindhoven	1	2–0
April 3rd 2007	PSV Eindhoven	1	3–0
Oct 24th 2007	Besiktas	1	1–2
Nov 6th 2007	Besiktas	1	8–0
Nov 28th 2007	Porto	1	4–1
Dec 11th 2007	Marseille	1	4–0
Feb 19th 2008	Inter Milan	1	2–0
April 8th 2008	Arsenal	1	4–2
Sept 9th 2008	Marseille	2	2–1
Oct 1st 2008	PSV Eindhoven	1	3–1
Nov 4th 2008	Atletico Madrid	1	1–1
Nov 26th 2008	Marseille	1	1–0
March 10th 2009	Real Madrid	2	4–0

— SPURS HAVE THAT SINKING FEELING —

On March 16th 1912, Tottenham came to Anfield for a First Division fixture and won 2–1. Less than a month later the *RMS Titanic* sunk in the north Atlantic. Spurs would not win again at Anfield for exactly 73 years when on March 16th 1985 a Garth Crooks winner stopped the rot.

— McLIVERPOOL —

Soon after the split with Everton FC, John Houlding appointed his friend John McKenna as full-time secretary of his new club and the new man quickly set about building what he hoped would be an all-conquering football team. McKenna, an Irishman, took his team on tour of Scotland and along the way recruited a squad of players that gave a particularly highland feel to the squad. In Liverpool's first ever league game against Middlesbrough Ironoplois in 1893, the club fielded seven players with surnames beginning Mc; hence the nickname the 'Team of Macs'.

These are the McPioneers:

Billy McOwen (goalkeeper)
Duncan McLean
Joe McQue
Jim McBride
James McVean (scored Liverpool's first ever league goal)
Matt McQueen
Hugh McQueen (Matt's brother)

The tradition continued in earnest with a number of Mc's starring for the Reds. Here's a selection:

Player	Seasons	Appearances	Goals
Terry McDermott	1974–1982	329	81
Steve McMahon	1985–1991	277	50
Gary McAllister	2000–2002	87	9
Steve McManaman	1992–1999	364	66
Jock McNab	1919–1928	222	6

— WHAT A SHOCKER —

Liverpool, like so many other clubs, have often come unstuck at the hands of an underdog in the FA Cup. Here are five embarrassing cup shocks:

Date	Opposition	Opp. Div.	Round	Score
Jan 15th 1959	Worcester City (A)	Southern lge	3rd	1–2
Feb 21st 1970	Watford (A)	2nd	6th	0–1
Feb 13th 1982	Chelsea (A)	2nd	5th	0–2
Jan 25th 1994	Bristol City (H)	1st	3rd	0–1
Jan 18th 2005	Burnley (A)	Championship	3rd	0–1

— THE FUTURE'S BRIGHT —

Liverpool's under-18 team have won the FA Youth Cup on three occasions.

Having lost over two legs in 1963 to West Ham, Liverpool's youngsters were second best again in 1972 when they lost 5–2 over two games to Aston Villa. However, when former winger Steve Heighway took over the youth set-up in 1989, progress began to be made. In 1996, Liverpool won their first Youth Cup and that progress has continued into the new millennium with the club winning back-to-back trophies in 2006 and 2007.

Here are the details of the club's three FA Youth Cup triumphs:

Year	Opposition	Aggregate Score
1996	West Ham United	4–1*
2006	Manchester City	3–2
2007	Manchester United	2–2 (3–2 on pens)

*Future first-team players Michael Owen, David Thompson and Jamie Carragher all starred in the win

— SAY IT AIN'T SO —

Every now and then an ex-Liverpool man has had the cheek to score against his old employers. Here's a selection of the ungrateful few:

Player	Date	New Team	Goals	Score
Jimmy Case	Feb 20th 1983	Brighton	1	1–2
Dean Saunders	Sep 19th 1992	Aston Villa	2	2–4
Peter Beardsley	Dec 7th 1992	Everton	1	1–2
Stan Collymore	Feb 28th 1998	Aston Villa	2	1–2
Robbie Fowler	Dec 28th 2003	Man City	1	2–2

— A LUCKY TROLL? —

Bob Paisley's success was not just down to shrewd management and spot on tactics. He also cited a lucky troll that he kept on his desk as a major reason for his side's unerring success under his stewardship. Paisley was given this troll by a Norwegian fan and its presence brought immediate luck, so it stayed in his office.

— A STATUE OF THE BOSS —

"He made the people happy"

On December 4th 1997, Liverpool Football Club unveiled an 8ft bronze statue of Bill Shankly outside the Kop end. The club were quite rightly honouring the man who brought them purpose, direction and ultimately glory.

The statue, by local artist Tom Murphy, was unveiled by Shankly's captain Ron Yeats and depicts the great man in familiar pose, arms aloft, lapping up the adulation from an adoring crowd.

Murphy used photos and footage of Shankly from 1973. The title just won, Shankly took to the field and walked to the Kop. One young fan threw his scarf onto the pitch and when an over-eager policeman went to kick it out of the way Shankly told the officer in no certain terms, "It's only a scarf to you, but it's that boy's life." Inscribed on the statue are simply the words: 'Bill Shankly – He Made the People Happy.'

— GREAT GAFFERS: GERARD HOULLIER —

Gerard Houllier was the first non-Liverpool man to take the manager's job at Anfield since Don Welsh in 1951. He would argue that he spent many happy afternoons on the Kop when working and living in Liverpool during the 1970s but that was as far as his connection with the club went.

Maybe that was a good thing. Liverpool needed to move into a new century and Houllier's knowledge of the European game and the methods needed to do well at the highest level made him a desirable choice. He immediately had to deal with the loss of Steve McManaman to Real Madrid on a free transfer before further breaking up the so-called 'Spice Boys' by selling David James, Jason McAteer and Paul Ince.

New foundations were built with the signings of centre-halves Sami Hyypia and Stephane Henchoz, while Dietmar Hamann was a fine addition to the midfield. In 1999/2000 Liverpool finished fourth but the fans had seen enough to think that trophies were at last more attainable.

Houllier remained active in the transfer market the following season. Emile Heskey arrived as a promising and bustling forward to challenge Robbie Fowler for the role of Michael Owen's partner, Nick Barmby made the short journey from Everton, Chrstian Ziege and Markus Babbel brought German know-how and Gary McAllister added poise, skill and experience to an evolving side that now included a young Steven Gerrard.

It was a cracking combination and while Houllier's team lacked the experience to win the Premiership, they gave the fans a season to remember with three cup victories in 2001 that will live long in the memory. Houllier's team looked capable of taking the title the following year but were shocked when, in October 2001, the manager was taken ill at half-time during a game at Anfield against Leeds. Houllier was told he needed life-saving heart surgery and took a sabbatical from the club. However, this worrying development seemed to galvanise the squad and under the caretaker leadership of Phil Thompson they enjoyed their best Premiership season, finishing a creditable second.

Houllier returned in March 2002 on an incredible night at Anfield when Liverpool needed to beat Roma by two goals to progress in the Champions League. With the Kop in full voice, Liverpool did just that. It was a magical occasion, but it was to prove a peak for Houllier as the side's fortunes started to slowly slide downhill.

Fans' confidence in the Frenchman's regime started to subside as new big money signings such as Bruno Cheyrou and El Hadji Diouf failed to deliver and what many saw as Houllier's over-cautious approach began to grate. A League Cup victory in 2003 over Manchester United bought the manager an extra season but, despite qualifying for the Champions League in 2004, it was once more time for a change.

It seems strange that despite relative success, Houllier's tenure is now frowned upon by some supporters. Possibly, the critics are disappointed that the great promise shown by his early team was never quite fulfilled. In time, though, Houllier will surely be remembered fondly as the man who gave Liverpool fans that heady spring of 2001.

Gerard Houllier fact-file

Games in charge   307 (plus 18 as joint manager with Roy Evans)

Honours	Seasons
League Cup	2000/01
FA Cup	2001
Uefa Cup	2000/01
Charity Shield	2001
League Cup	2003

— HICKSON CONTROVERSY

A player swapping Red for Blue and vice versa can cause a stink but none more so than Liverpool's signing of Everton's David Hickson in 1959. Hickson, blond, dashing and the hero of Goodison, was snapped up by the Reds but the signing had both Kopites and Evertonians alike threatening to tear up their season tickets.

Hickson was a deadly striker who, because he was so adored by Evertonians was a figure of hate among Kopites. For the hardcore, the thought of him at 30 years old suddenly becoming a Red was simply too much.

Liverpool, however, were floundering in the Second Division and needed Hickson's firepower. And despite the threats, a bumper 50,000 crowd turned up to see the new boy's debut at Anfield. Hickson, of course, scored two goals in a 2–1 win over Aston Villa, got a kiss from one fan and went on to get 38 goals in just 67 games.

— WINNING THE LEAGUE ON THE RADIO —

1946/47 had been a strange season. For seven years, football had been held up by war and now at the end of the campaign, Liverpool fans and players would have another wait on their hands to discover just how well they had done. A long, harsh winter had disrupted the season and meant that Liverpool played their last league game on the last day of May. George Kay's men had famously won at Wolves, meaning that Stoke had to win their last game at Sheffield United to take the championship on goal-difference. The agonising thing for Liverpool's fans was that the game at Bramall Lane wasn't for two weeks.

By chance, on the day Stoke finally took to the field in Yorkshire, Liverpool were entertaining Everton in the final of Liverpool's Senior Cup. More than 40,000 fans came to Anfield but most had their minds on what was happening across the Pennines where Sheffield United took an early lead but were soon pegged back by a Stoke goal.

The Liverpool players were well aware of what was going on but managed to concentrate and take a 2–1 lead. Soon, so did Sheffield United and with five minutes left of the match at Anfield, the Liverpool chairman, Bill McConnell came on the tannoy and announced that Stoke had lost and Liverpool were champions.

Centre half, Laurie Hughes takes up the story. "We'd done it. There was a huge roar, one that would have rivalled Hampden Park and hats were thrown into the air by the thousands of fans packed into Anfield. Both teams stopped playing and we were rewarded with a handshake from our Evertonian opponents before celebrating in the centre-circle with a happy huddle. We carried on playing mind, we had some defending to do."

Laurie and his mates held on and won the Senior Cup as well.

— LIVERPOOL, LIVERPOOL, LIVERPOOL —

Liverpool celebrated it's 800th year as a city in 2007. Since 1207, plenty of other towns and city have been named after the original. Here they are:

Liverpool, Nova Scotia, Canada	Founded 1759
Liverpool, New York, USA	Founded 1797
Liverpool, Pennsylvania, USA	Founded 1808
Liverpool, New South Wales, Australia	Founded 1810
Liverpool, Ohio, USA	Founded 1816
Liverpool, Texas, USA	Founded 1837

— GREAT GAFFERS: ROY EVANS —

"He's too nice." That was what the critics said of Roy Evans when his managerial tenure came to an end at Anfield in 1998. Yes, Evans was an amiable man; yes, he did sometimes struggle in the new world of football that saw players treated like superstars, but to say he was too nice for the job is to over-simplify his reign.

Evans was the perfect man for the job. Not only had he been at Liverpool for years (he played 11 times for the club before injury ended his career at the age of 25), not only had he worked with the reserves and the first team since 1975, but he was also the man who could stabilise the ship after Graeme Souness' choppy time at the wheel. Evans immediately got the players smiling again, he adopted a new 3-5-2 formation built around the exciting Steve McManaman and soon Liverpool were challenging for honours once more. In 1995 his team won the League Cup, with a Wembley victory over Bolton, and more success seemed likely.

McManaman, Robbie Fowler, Rob Jones and Jamie Redknapp were gelling with older heads Ian Rush, John Barnes and Mark Wright and the following season promised much. Promise, though, would be a label too often stuck on Evans' sides. While they played easily the best football seen at Anfield during the 1990s, the team lacked the belief and aggression shown by Manchester United, the dominant club at the time. The 1996 FA Cup final between the two sides highlighted this fact, with Alex Ferguson's men stealing the trophy despite both teams' poor showing.

Evans tried to make amends, but despite a good showing in the Premiership Liverpool's challenge to United in 1996/97, fell short three-quarters of the way through. He tried to shore things up with the signing of Paul Ince and later the emergence of Michael Owen brought goals, but the momentum of his early years had been lost. In the summer of 1998 the Liverpool board acted, deciding to bring in a new man to 'share' the job.

Roy Evans fact-file

Games in charge	226 (plus 18 as joint manager with Gerard Houllier)

Honours	Seasons
League Cup	1994/95

— LIVERPOOL'S FIRST EUROPEAN ADVENTURE —

Having won the league in 1964, Liverpool and Bill Shankly prepared for the first of many exciting forays into the uncharted territory of the European Cup. Their first test would, as if to underline how adventurous the continental game could be, take them to Reykjavik, Iceland.

In August 1964, Liverpool Football Club departed the city for foreign climbs for the first time. The Reds flew from Manchester to Glasgow and from there took a bus to Renfrew where they connected with a flight to the Icelandic capital. Shankly was keen on breaking up the journey so took his team for a few hours to a holiday camp in Ayr.

As the bus arrived at the gates of the camp, Shankly leant out of the window and called to the gateman. "This is Liverpool Football Club – on their way to Iceland." To which the unimpressed gateman replied, "Aye, well you've taken the wrong road!"

For the record, Liverpool won the game 5–0, thanks to two goals from Gordon Wallace and Roger Hunt and one from Phil Chisnall.

— LIVERPOOL'S INTERNATIONAL DOUBLE WINNERS —

The Liverpool side that beat Everton on May 10th 1986 to win the Reds' one and only League and FA Cup Double did not include a single player eligible to play for England. Mark Lawrenson was born and bred in Lancashire but played for the Republic of Ireland and otherwise, the players hailed from Australia to Zimbabwe.

Here are the double winners and the countries they played (or could play) for:

Bruce Grobbelaar	Zimbabwe
Steve Nicol	Scotland
Alan Hansen	Scotland
Mark Lawrenson	Republic of Ireland
Jim Beglin	Republic of Ireland
Craig Johnston	Australia or South Africa
Kevin McDonald	Scotland
Jan Molby	Denmark
Ronnie Whelan	Republic of Ireland
Kenny Dalglish	Scotland
Ian Rush	Wales

— SCOUSE XI —

Kopites have had many local heroes to cheer on over the years. Here's the pick of the bunch:

John Whitehead (goalkeeper)*
1895–1896
Apps: 3

Tommy Smith	**Jamie Carragher**	**Phil Thompson**	**Gerry Byrne**
1963–1978	1997–	1972–1985	1957–1969
Apps: 638	Apps: 577	Apps: 477	Apps: 333
Goals: 48	Goals: 5	Goals: 13	Goals: 4

Ian Callaghan	**Jimmy Case**	**Steven Gerrard**	**Steve McManaman**
1960–1978	1975–1981	1998–	1990–1999
Apps: 857	Apps: 269	Apps: 483	Apps: 364
Goals: 68	Goals: 46	Goals: 120	Goals: 66

Robbie Fowler	**John Aldridge**
1993–01 & 06–07	1987–1989
Apps: 369	Apps: 104
Goals: 183	Goals: 63

Subs: **Sammy Lee** (1978–1986, 295/19), **Steve McMahon** (1985–1991, 277/50), **David Fairclough** (1975–1983, 154/55)

Manager: **Joe Fagan**

* Scouse goalkeepers who have regularly played for Liverpool are very hard to come by. Whitehead was the first of just a few to keep goal for the club.

— DON'T MENTION THE WAR, SAINT —

On June 6th 1964 Liverpool played German side MSV Duisburg in Vancouver Canada as part of a post-season tour to North America. The game was to commemorate the twentieth anniversary of the D-Day landings and while the game finished in an amicable 1–1 draw (Liverpool's goal was scored by Alf Arrowsmith) Ian St John (along with a German opponent) was sent off.

— THIS IS ANFIELD —

The exact date that manager Bill Shankly had the 'This is Anfield' sign put up above the players' tunnel is not known, but it is thought to be during the 1960/61 season.

Legend has it that an opposing player was heard by Bill Shankly asking a team-mate, "Where exactly are we playing today?" The sign was a reminder that the opposition were entering into one of the most intimidating venues in British football. The current sign is the third since the original.

— THE LAST TO CROSS THE GREAT DIVIDE —

Transfers between Liverpool and Everton raise eyebrows but they do happen. When it comes, though, to Liverpool doing business with Manchester United you have to go back a long way to find a player who has made the move. It was April 1964. Phil Chisnall, a Mancunian forward who had helped United win the 1963 FA Cup joined Liverpool for the then large fee of £25,000. Chisnall, despite scoring in Liverpool's first ever European Cup tie in Iceland, didn't make an impact for the Reds, playing just nine games, scoring twice.

— THE WORLD CLUB CHAMPIONSHIPS —

Despite having won the European Cup five times, Liverpool are yet to be crowned as World Club champions. The title fought out between the champions of South America and Europe used to be played over two legs and in both 1977 and 1978 Liverpool declined to take part. The often overly physical fixtures coupled with the long flights were off-putting to the club but once it was moved to a one-off game in Tokyo in 1980, the Reds opted to give it a go.

Date	Opposition	Score
December 13th 1981	Flamengo (Brazil)	0–3
December 9th 1984	Independiente (Argentina)	0–1
December 18th 2005	Sao Paulo (Brazil)	0–1*

*By 2005 Fifa had changed the format from a one-off game to a mini-tournament in which the winners from all five confederations participated. Liverpool played Costa Rican club Deportivo Saprissa in the semi-final and won 3–0.

— THEY CALL IT MELLOW YELLOW —

In recent years Liverpool have often sported a yellow away kit. In fact, the away shirts worn in the 2006/07 season were yellow and going back to the 1990s and the 1980s Liverpool often wore yellow on their travels. The first time, though, that the club wore yellow was actually at Anfield.

Ajax of Amsterdam (whose classic red and white strip clashed with both Liverpool's traditional red and white shirts) were the visitors in a European Cup first round second leg clash in 1966. Johan Cruyff scored twice in a 2–2 draw but the Dutch won 7–3 on aggregate.

The yellow jersey wasn't worn again until March 31st 1979 in an FA Cup semi-final against Manchester United at Maine Road. Again the final score was 2–2.

— FIRST ENGLAND SKIPPER —

Emlyn Hughes did it with distinction, Ray Clemence did it, Steven Gerrard has done it but the first Liverpool player to captain England was solid right-back Ephraim Longworth who, on May 21st 1921, skippered the national team for the first and only time against Belgium in Brussels.

— THE BEST OF BRITISH —

Since playing their first major European game in 1964, Liverpool have faced other British sides on 18 occasions, losing five of the ties:

Season	Opposition	Competition	Aggregate score
1964/65	Celtic (Sc)	Cup Winners Cup	2–1
1970/71	Hibernian Sc)	Fairs Cup	3–0
1970/71	Leeds	Fairs Cup	0–1
1972/73	Tottenham	Uefa Cup	2–2*
1975/76	Hibernian (Sc)	Uefa Cup	3–2
1976/77	Crusaders (NI)	European Cup	7–0
1978/79	Nottingham Forest	European Cup	0–2
1980/81	Aberdeen (Sc)	European Cup	5–0
1997/98	Celtic (Sc)	Uefa Cup	2–2*
2002/03	Celtic (Sc)	Uefa Cup	1–3
2004/05	Chelsea	Champions League	1–0
2005/06	Total Network Sol (W)	Champions League	6–0
2005/06	Chelsea	Champions League+	0–0
2005/06	Chelsea	Champions League+	0–0
2006/07	Chelsea	Champions League	1–1^
2007/08	Arsenal	Champions League	5–3
2007/08	Chelsea	Champions League	3–4
2008/09	Chelsea	Champions League	5–7

* Won on away goals
^ Won 4–1 on penalties
+ Group Stage

— LIVERPOOL'S BEST EVER START TO A SEASON —

On March 16th 1988, a Craig Johnston goal earned Liverpool a 1–1 draw at Derby. Not only did that point take the Reds a step closer to their 17th League Championship, it sealed the club's 29th game unbeaten from the start of a remarkable season.

Kenny Dalglish had spent the previous summer strengthening his squad and a new-look forward line of John Aldridge, Peter Beardsley and John Barnes enabled Liverpool to play some of the best football ever seen at Anfield. The 29 games unbeaten also equalled Leeds United's record set in the 1973/74 season but, alas, defeat at Goodson Park the following Sunday meant there was no outright record.

If you do find yourself arguing the merits of each run with a Leeds fan, they won 19 and drew 10 of their games, while Liverpool won 22 and drew just 7. In 2003/04, Arsenal outdid both clubs and went the whole Premiership season unbeaten.

— GERRY'S PAIN IN THE NECK —

Three minutes into the 1965 FA Cup final, Liverpool full back Gerry Byrne went into a heavy tackle with Leeds' hard man Bobby Collins, fell awkwardly and lay prostrate on the Wembley turf. Bill Shankly immediately sent his trainer Bob Paisley onto the pitch to check the damage. Just minutes earlier Shankly had told his team to go out and die for the fans who had flocked to London but watching Byrne getting treatment, he must have been cursing his whole-hearted full back for taking him a little too literally.

Bob Paisley had an uncanny knack of quickly diagnosing an injury and having had a feel of Byrne's collarbone immediately knew that it was broken. These, though, were the days before substitutes and Byrne insisted he could carry on and so he did, making sure that neither Paisley or his manager told the rest of the team about the extent of his injury for fear that the Leeds players would find out and, as ever, show little mercy.

The game itself was a stalemate but Gerry Byrne played on and on and on, keeping Leeds' Johnny Giles quiet and even finding the energy early in extra-time to burst down the left wing, receive the ball from Peter Thompson and cross for Roger Hunt to open the scoring. Leeds equalised but an Ian St John effort brought the FA Cup to Liverpool for the first time. Byrne was quite rightly hailed a hero and three days later, his arm in a sling, it was Byrne (and the also injured Gordon Milne) who paraded the cup around Anfield before the European Cup semi-final against Inter Milan.

— VE VON ZE LEAGUE! —

With the war just over in the summer of 1945, Liverpool travelled to Germany to play the RAF and the Combined Services in a morale boosting tour. On arrival the club received as a gift a set of brand, spanking new red shirts which they gleefully accepted due to the shortage of good material and clothing back in post-war England. The shirts, though, had sinister origins as they had been made from the hundreds of red Nazi flags pulled down by the allies at the end of the hostilities. Liverpool took the shirts home with them, played the 1945/46 season in them and it is thought they wore the same tops when they claimed the first League Championship title after the war.

— THE OTHER TWO —

Liverpool's first forays into continental finals came not in the European Cup but in its smaller cousins.

The Reds never won the old Cup Winners Cup, but they were beaten finalists in 1966, when they lost 2–1 to Borussia Dortmund at Hampden Park just weeks before England beat Germany in the World Cup final at Wembley.

Liverpool's first European success came in 1973 in the Uefa Cup, formerly the Inter City Fairs Cup. It is a competition that has been good to Liverpool and three different managers.

Liverpool's Uefa and Cup Winners' Cup finals are:

Cup	Date	Opponents and Venue	Score
CWC	May 5th 1966	Borussia Dortmund (Hampden Park)	1–2 (aet)
Uefa	May 10th 1973	Borussia Moenchengladbach (H)	3–0 (1st leg)
Uefa	May 23rd 1973	Borussia Moenchengladbach (A)	0–2 (2nd leg)
Uefa	April 28th 1976	Bruges (H)	3–2 (1st leg)
Uefa	May 19th 1976	Bruges (A)	1–1 (2nd leg)
Uefa	May 16th 2001	Alaves (Dortmund)	5–4 (aet)

— LIVERPOOL'S YOUNGEST EVER PLAYER —

The FA Cup bunting was still up, the pubs still reeling from another FA Cup win. May 8th 1974, just four days after the Reds had trounced (yes trounced) Newcastle 3–0 at Wembley in the cup final, Liverpool had to travel down to Tottenham's White Hart Lane to play the final game of the season.

Bill Shankly made one change to the team that had won at Wembley, bringing in reserve team defender Max Thompson for centre-forward John Toshack. Thompson was 17-years-old and 129 days when he took to the field as Liverpool youngest ever player, a record that still stands today. Thompson didn't do badly as Liverpool earned a 1–1 draw but little did anyone know at the time that the match at Spurs would be the last Bill Shankly would ever pick as Liverpool boss. Shankly resigned just weeks later and under new manager Bob Paisley, Thompson made only one more appearance in a second round Uefa Cup tie at Anfield against Real Sociedad. Just over a year later, in December 1977, Thompson left for Blackpool but he still remains the true baby of the Liverpool team.

— INTERNATIONAL REDS —

Over the years Liverpool have fielded many internationals. While most of them have been from the three home nations and the Republic of Ireland, there have been plenty of other international caps won by players from all over the world. Spain has the most representatives with seven:

Country	Player
Argentina	Javier Mascherano
Australia	Harry Kewell
Brazil	Lucas Leiva
Cameroon	Rigobert Song
Chile	Mark Gonzalez
Croatia	Igor Biscan
Czech Republic	Vladimir Smicer, Patrik Berger, Milan Baros
Denmark	Jan Molby, Torben Piechnik, Daniel Agger
Finland	Sami Hyypia, Jari Litmanen
France	Nicolas Anelka, Bruno Cheyrou, Djibril Cisse, Alou Diarra*
Germany	Dietmar Hamann, Christian Ziege
Holland	Sander Westerveld, Dirk Kuyt, Ryan Babel
Hungary	Istvan Kozma
Israel	Avi Cohen, Ronny Rosenthal, Yossi Benayoun
Italy	Andrea Dossena
Mali	Djimi Traore, Mohamed Sissoko
Morocco	Nabil El Zhar
Norway	Vegard Heggem, Stig Bjornebye, Oyvind Leonhardsen, John Arne Riise
Poland	Jerzy Dudek
Portugal	Abel Xavier
Senegal	El Hadji Diouf, Salif Diao
Slovakia	Martin Skrtel
South Africa	Arthur Riley
Spain	Xabi Alonso, Sanz Luis Garcia, Fernando Morientes, Jose Reina, Fernando Torres, Alvaro Arbeloa, Albert Riera
Sweden	Glenn Hysen
Switzerland	Stephane Henchoz
Ukraine	Andriy Voronin
USA	Brad Friedel
Zimbabwe	Bruce Grobbelaar

*Alou Diarra won his France cap while on loan at Lyon

— RED LEGENDS: KENNY DALGLISH —

King Kenny

What did the fans love most about Kenny Dalglish? The goals, the skill, the team-work, the trophies? They all helped, but it might just be a lot simpler than that. When Kenny Dalglish scored a goal, there was no moody expression, no arrogant finger to the mouth to silence the opposing supporters. There was just a smile, a big beaming smile that told of a player doing what he loved best, and doing it absolutely brilliantly.

Kenny Dalglish – much to Bill Shankly's annoyance later – came to Liverpool as a schoolboy but was deemed not good enough. Instead he went to Celtic and scored 167 goals before Bob Paisley rectified the club's previous error and spent £440,000 to bring him south of the border.

Liverpool fans were wondering about the future. Sure they were the new champions of Europe but their talismanic striker Kevin Keegan had left the club. Paisley looked to Dalglish. The manager later said that even had Keegan stayed he would have brought Dalglish to the club. "Who knows," he joked, " I might have won something then."

It was soon a case of "Kevin who?" Dalglish scored on his league debut at Middlesbrough, he scored the sixth in a 6–0 win over Keegan's Hamburg in the European Super Cup and then that May he scored a wonderful goal at Wembley to win the European Cup final against Bruges.

In all, he got 32 goals that first season at the club and a new hero was born. Dalglish, along with fellow Scots Alan Hansen and Graeme Souness, helped Paisley's new team look even better than the old one. They slowly became the most successful side in the modern game, and Dalglish was their most influential player.

In the early part of the 1980s his partnership with Ian Rush was perhaps the best the English game has ever seen as trophy after trophy settled into the Anfield trophy cabinet. Dalglish had never been captain of Liverpool but in 1985 it was he who the board turned to to replace the retiring Joe Fagan.

Dalglish's appointment as player-manager raised more than a few eyebrows but while it looked like his boots may be hung up in favour of the managerial tracksuit it became clear that in order to keep the silver polish in use, his skills on the pitch were still very necessary. His very presence took Liverpool to the Double in his first season in charge.

He was officially a Liverpool player until 1990 but by then his legs were no longer able to carry the genius footballing brain. By then, he had won three league titles as manager. Was there nothing he couldn't do for the club?

Dalglish was at home leading the attack as he was dropping deep. He could pass, he could compete, he could shoot from long-range, he could sniff out a chance in the penalty box. In 1983 at Arsenal, after a stirring Liverpool move he dummied one defender, took one touch to make space for a shot and curled the ball with his left foot into the top corner past Pat Jennings. It was a piece of sheer brilliance followed by that brilliant smile. When it comes to King Kenny, the fans today remind anyone who'll listen of the best they've ever seen. "And Could He Play!" He certainly could.

Kenny Dalglish fact-file

Appearances	511
Goals	172
Scotland caps while at Liverpool	54

Honours	Season
First Division Championship	1978/79
	1979/80
	1981/82
	1982/83
	1983/84
	1985/86
FA Cup	1986
League Cup	1980/81
	1981/82
	1982/83
	1983/84
European Cup	1977/78
	1980/81
	1983/84
Charity Shield	1977*
	1979
	1980
	1986*
Football Writers Player of the Year	1979
1983	
PFA Player of the Year	1983

*Shared

— SHANKS PLAYS FOR LIVERPOOL —

Think Bill Shankly and you think of the man in the suit, inspiring his players from the sidelines. Ask the older generation and they will tell you of Shankly the player, a steely half-back with a rock hard tackle and a will to win that he soon would demand from his players.

Bill Shankly won five pre-war caps for Scotland and an FA Cup winners' medal in 1938 for Preston (where today he is still fondly remembered, so much so that a stand is named after him).

During the war, however, Shankly turned out as a guest for Liverpool, the club he would one day make great. It was May 30th 1942, Everton were the visitors at Anfield in a wartime fixture that saw Shankly pull on the red jersey for the only time. Always fiercely competitive, Shankly was at his solid best, helping Liverpool to a 4–1 win over their neighbours thanks to goals from Cyril Done (2), Len Carney and JE Wharton. Unfortunately, there were only 13,761 fans there to see it.

— LIFE, DEATH AND MORE IMPORTANT THINGS —

"This city has two great football teams –
Liverpool and Liverpool reserves."

"I know you're there . . . you're spying on us. Why don't you come out, you cowards?"
Bill Shankly to a light bulb in an Eastern Europe hotel room

"Chairman Mao has never seen a greater show of red strength than today."
Bill Shankly about the fans after the 1974 FA Cup final win over Newcastle

"I've never seen any of The Beatles standing on the Kop and any tickets I have spare will be going to my mates on the Kop."
Bill Shankly responds to a request from Beatles manager Brian Epstein for tickets before the 1965 FA Cup final

"What do you mean your knee? That's Liverpool's knee."
Bill Shankly to Tommy Smith when his player complained of a dodgy knee

"I'll have to find someone else for the reserves."
Bill Shankly after Lou Macari turned down Liverpool for Manchester United

"If Tommy Smith isn't named Footballer of the Year, then football should be stopped and the men who pick any other player sent to the Kremlin. I understand it isn't a very sociable place."
Bill Shankly in 1971 – Smith didn't win the award

"My idea was to build Liverpool into a bastion of invincibility. Napoleon had that idea. He would conquer the bloody world. Liverpool would be untouchable. My idea was to build Liverpool up and up until eventually everybody would have to submit, to give in."
Bill Shankly

"Your trouble son, is that your brains are all in your head."
Bill Shankly to a young player

"Spurs? Cockney tap dancers more like."
Bill Shankly on the White Hart Lane club

— THE INVINCIBLES —

The next time you hear an Arsenal fan crowing about their 2003/04 unbeaten league run, tell them that going a whole season without defeat is so 1894!

Liverpool's first season in league football saw them go the entire campaign in the old Second Division unbeaten. They won 22 of their 28 games (including all 14 at Anfield) and drew six, scoring 77 and conceding just 18 and easily gained promotion to the First Division.

— ONE CAP WONDERS —

Seven players have won just the one cap for England while playing their football for Liverpool. These are the one cap wonders:

Player	Date	Opposition
Tom Bradshaw	February 20th 1897	Ireland
Frank Becton	March 29th 1897	Wales
'Rabbi' Howell	April 8th 1899	Scotland
John Bamber	March 14th 1921	Wales
Tommy Smith	May 19th 1971	Wales
Neil Ruddock	November 16th 1994	Nigeria
David James	March 29th 1997	Mexico

— FINAL WOES —

Considering Liverpool's long and illustrious history, the 12 defeats the Reds have suffered in major finals is not a bad return. Apologies to those who were keen to forget these occasions, but here they are anyway:

Date	Competition	Opposition	Score
April 25th 1914	FA Cup	Burnley	0–1
April 29th 1950	FA Cup	Arsenal	0–2
May 5th 1966	Cup Winners Cup	Borussia Dortmund	1–2 (aet)
May 8th 1971	FA Cup	Arsenal	1–2 (aet)
May 21st 1977	FA Cup	Manchester United	1–2
March 22nd 1978	League Cup	Nottingham Forest	0–1*
May 29th 1985	European Cup	Juventus	0–1
April 5th 1987	League Cup	Arsenal	1–2
May 14th 1988	FA Cup	Wimbledon	0–1
May 17th 1996	FA Cup	Manchester United	0–1
February 27th 2005	League Cup	Chelsea	2–3 (aet)
May 23rd 2007	Champions League	AC Milan	1–2

*Liverpool lost to Nottingham Forest at Old Trafford in a replay after a 0–0 draw at Wembley

— AN ODD PRESENT FOR BILLY —

On November 9th 1957 Billy Liddell ran out at Anfield to face Notts County in what was his 430th game for the club, one more than Elisha Scott and a new Liverpool record. To mark the occasion, the County players all lined up in the centre circle to shake the great player's hand and the club bought their flying forward a brand new cocktail cabinet. A strange choice as Billy was teetotal!

— PEPE'S GOT MORE CLEAN SHEETS THAN M&S! —

On April 21st 2007, Pepe Reina made his 100th appearance for Liverpool against Wigan and kept his 55th clean sheet, giving the Spaniard more shut-outs in his first 100 games than any other Liverpool goalkeeper in history. He beat Ray Clemence who kept 51 clean sheets in his first 100 games, Bruce Grobbelaar who kept 50 and Jerzey Dudek who kept 45.

At the end of the 2007/08 season Pepe picked up the Barclays Golden Glove Award. The gong is given to the Premier League keeper with the most clean sheets in the season and for the third successive season, Liverpool's reliable last line of defence romped home with 18 shut-outs. Portsmouth's former Red David James came second with 15.

— EL RED MEN —

Before June 2004, Liverpool had never had a Spaniard in the team but when Rafa Benitez took over as manager that all changed. Since then three Spanish players have played 100 games for the club:

Player	100th game for the club
Luis Garcia	September 20th 2006 v Newcastle at Anfield (2–0)
Xabi Alonso	October 28th 2006 v Aston Villa at Anfield (3–1)
Jose Reina	April 21st 2007 v Wigan at Anfield (2–0)

— A DENT IN THE CELEBRATIONS —

After the amazing events in Istanbul on May 25th 2005, it was little wonder that the Liverpool players' celebrations were on the raucous side. The next time you visit the Anfield trophy cabinet take a closer look at the trophy won that night in Turkey. There is a dent on one of the handles caused by an unnamed player dropping the famous piece of silverware. Liverpool decided not to have it fixed (after all, they didn't have to give it back as they had won it for a fifth time), thinking the mark on the cup only enhanced the memories of the legendary occasion.

— STEVIE G.A.Y. —

Liverpool captain Steven Gerrard was voted top of the Gay Football Supporters Network 2006 'Lust List'. In 2008, Fernando Torres took the same honour.

— THE SECOND YOUNGEST TO GET HIS HANDS ON BIG EARS! —

When, on May 25th 2005, just five days shy of his 25th birthday, Steven Gerrard lifted the Champions League up toward the Turkish night sky, he became the youngest British captain to lift the trophy. In fact, only Didier Deschamps who led Marseille to victory in 1993 is a younger winning captain in the history of the European Cup.

— RUSH'S SHEVA GIFT —

In 1990, Dynamo Kiev brought a team to Wales to compete in the Ian Rush Cup. At the end of the youth tournament Rush awarded a pair of his old boots to the young boy who finished the tournament as top goalscorer. That 14-year-old was a young boy in the Kiev side. His name? Andrei Shevchenko.

— A SPOOKY RED —

Fans of Living TV's Derek Acorah will be fascinated to find out that the renowned television psychic and medium from Bootle was on the books at Liverpool while Bill Shankly was the manager. He played a few games for the reserves but never appeared for the first team.

— ALDO'S ALMOST SPOT ON —

Think John Aldridge and penalties and you immediately think of the one he missed against Wimbledon at Wembley in the 1988 FA Cup final. That's harsh, though. In the two and a half seasons Aldridge spent at Anfield, Aldridge took 18 penalties and the one saved by Wimbledon's Dave Beasant is the only one he missed. The other 17 were all perfectly put away and he even signed off with a penalty kick when he came on against Crystal Palace on September 12th 1989, scoring from the spot with his first touch and bidding farewell to the Kop during the 9–0 demolition of the south Londoners.

— A EUROPEAN CUP WON ON THE ROAD —

Liverpool's European Cup win of 1983/84 was possibly the hardest fought considering the places the team had to visit and the results they required. The campaign started with a relatively easy trip to Denmark's Odense but from there it was all uphill and culminated with a victorious final in Rome against Roma!

Round Two

Atletico Bilbao (h)	First leg	0–0
Atletico Bilbao (a)	Second leg	1–0

Round Three

Benfica (h)	First leg	1–0
Benfica (a)	Second leg	4–1

Semi-final

Dinamo Bucharest (h	First leg	1–0
Dinamo Bucharest (a)	Second leg	2–1

— THE SCOREBOARD DOESN'T LIE (ALWAYS) —

Before the Merseyside derby at Anfield on the last day of January 2004, the scoreboard made an error and announced the score as LIVERPOOL 54, EVERTON 0. Rush got one, Rush got two . . .

— SISTER ACT —

The Kemlyn Road Stand at Anfield was built in 1963 and housed 6,600 fans. In the late 1970s and early 1980s the club began buying the houses on Kemlyn Road in the hope that they could re-develop the stand and increase the capacity. Those plans, however, were put on hold until 1990 because two sisters, Joan and Nora Mason refused to sell their house until then. Only after an agreement had finally been reached with the two sisters could the club set about demolishing the houses and developing what is now the Centenary Stand.

— THE NOT SO CHARITY SHIELD —

The 1974 Charity Shield was a match of firsts. It was the first Charity Shield to be held at Wembley, it was the first Liverpool team to be picked by new manager Bob Paisley (although as a mark of respect, Bill Shankly was asked to lead the team out for one last game), and it was Brian Clough's first game in charge of Leeds (he only stayed for 44 days, mind).

Even more memorably, though, it was a game in which the first British players were sent off at Wembley and, at the end of a 1–1 draw, it was the first time Liverpool had ever contested a penalty shoot-out.

The main talking point was the dismissals. Don Revie's Leeds had been far from shrinking violets and, despite a new man at the helm in Clough, their physical approach remained at the fore. Kevin Keegan had been singled out for some especially rough tactics and when on the hour he was clattered into by Johnny Giles, enough was enough.

Keegan had been sent off just four days earlier in a pre-season friendly and once more the red mist descended. Unfortunately, that red mist must have somewhat blinded the little striker as he immediately made a beeline for Billy Bremner thinking it was the Scot who had kicked him rather than Giles. To be fair to Keegan, Bremner had been trying to intimidate him all afternoon but it was still a surprise to see the striker throw a punch at the Leeds captain.

What followed was a playground brawl and both Keegan and Bremner were shown the red card. To add insult to injury, both players tore off their shirts while walking off – a gesture of disrespect that infuriated the watching FA bigwigs. Both Keegan and Bremner were subsequently fined £500 and banned for 11 matches each.

Back on the pitch, meanwhile, Liverpool won the shoot-out.

— A GAYLE BLOWS THROUGH MUNICH —

Toxteth-born Howard Gayle made his debut for Liverpool as a substitute on October 4th 1980 in a league game against Manchester City. He went on to make just five appearances for the club, but one of those run-outs was instrumental in Liverpool's path to a third European Cup.

The Reds had been drawn against Bayern Munich in the semi-final and when the Germans earned a 0–0 draw at Anfield, they were clearly ecstatic with a result they felt would be more than enough to take them to the final in Paris. The German mood was lifted further with the news that Bob Paisley's defence had been depleted by injuries to Alan Kennedy and captain Phil Thompson. This was going to be tough for the English champions. They still had the likes of Kenny Dalglish but he was immediately singled out in the second leg, kicked heavily early on and forced to limp off after just nine minutes. His replacement was the 23-year-old striker Gayle who, if he was daunted by the occasion, the 75,000 fans or the huge Olympic stadium in Munich, hid it amazingly well.

Gayle (Liverpool's first ever black player) set about a German defence boasting internationals such as Klaus Augenthaler at centre-back and was immediately in their faces, running them into the corners, disrupting any rhythm they tried to gain. He was, of course, harshly treated by the defenders but he got on with his job until the 70th minute when those rough tackles finally took their toll and he was replaced by Jimmy Case. Thirteen minutes later, stand-in skipper Ray Kennedy scored and despite a late Karl-Heinze Rumminegge goal, Liverpool were through on the away goal. It was a famous night in which Gayle had more than played his part.

— GOLDEN SHANKS —

By the early 1970s Bill Shankly had become one of the most famous and respected men in European football and so adidas decided they wanted to award the great man with one of their Golden Boots. The boots are made to fit the recipient's feet perfectly so adidas called Anfield to find out Shankly's shoe size. Bob Paisley took the call and turned to Shanks. "Bill, it's adidas. They're making you a golden boot, what size are you?"

"If it's real gold,' replied Shankly, "I'm a size 28!"

— THE FIELDS OF ANFIELD ROAD —

Sung to the tune of 'Fields of Athenry' and accredited to Liverpool
Away Supporters Club in the late 1990s:

Outside the Shankly Gates
I heard a Kopite calling
Shankly they have taken you away
But you left the greatest eleven
Just before they took you to heaven
And the redmen, are still playing the same old way

All round the Fields of Anfield Road
Where once we watched the King Kenny play (and could he play)
We had Heighway on the wing
We had dreams and songs to sing
Of the glory, round the Fields of Anfield Road

Outside the Paisley Gates
I heard a Kopite calling
Paisley they have taken you away
You led the great 11
Back in Rome in 77
And the redmen, are still playing the same old way

All round the Fields of Anfield Road
Where once we watched the King Kenny play (and could he play)
We had Heighway on the wing
We had dreams and songs to sing
Of the glory round the Fields of Anfield Road

— SOLID DEFENCE —

During their triumphant 1978/79 league season, Liverpool conceded
just 16 goals (a total that included just four at Anfield). It was a record
that stood until 2004/05 when Chelsea let in only 15 goals. Would it
be churlish to remind everyone that Liverpool played 42 games while
Chelsea played just 38?

— FA CUPS DOUBLE —

In 2006 Liverpool became one of only four clubs to have won both
the FA Cup and the FA Youth Cup in the same season, along with
Arsenal (1971), Everton (1984) and Coventry City (1987).

— IT'S A FIX! —

Today the very thought of Liverpool and Manchester United players meeting for a pint and planning anything together is ludicrous, but back in 1915 it actually happened, and with far from happy consequences.

Britain was at war, a bloody war that looked like going on and on. Subsequently, the 1914/15 league campaign took on a hollow feel. That said, Manchester United were struggling at the bottom of the table and needed favours to stay up. Those favours came from the rather strange source of Anfield. Money was tight and so a group of Liverpool players met some of their United counterparts in a Manchester pub and hatched a plan that they hoped would make them all a bit of money, as well as earning United some valuable points.

The two teams were due to meet on Good Friday at Old Trafford and the players decided they could agree a scoreline, make sure sufficient funds were put down at as many bookmakers as possible and collect the cash. The game itself was a farce. United won 2–0 but Liverpool were so poor that alarm bells were immediately raised. Liverpool missed chance after chance, missed a penalty and when it emerged that a lot of money had gone down on that exact result, it was no surprise when the bookmakers complained and refused to pay out and then the Football League decided to investigate further.

The truth soon came out and four Liverpool players – Jackie Sheldon, Tom Miller, Tom Fairfoul and Bob Purcell – were found guilty of their crime. They, along with four United players (including ex-Liverpool man, Enoch 'Knocker' West) were suspended from playing indefinitely. Seven of the players were allowed back straight after the war but West, who unlike the others protested his innocence, had to wait much longer. Eventually, his ban was lifted in 1945 – when he was 62!

— A HAT-TRICK OF TITLES —

Having lost their title to Aston Villa in 1981, Liverpool took stock and went on to win the League Championship for the next three seasons. Their hat-trick of titles from 1982 to 1984 was the first time a club had achieved that feat since Arsenal (1933–35) and Huddersfield (1924–26). Manchester United have since replicated the achievement, winning the Premiership from 1999 to 2001 and 2007 to 2009.

— SIX SHORT MINUTES —

The start of the second half of the 2005 Champions League final suggested there would be no miracle. Milan came out for the second half as they had finished the first and it was they who looked more likely to score next. Jerzy Dudek made a great save from a free-kick and almost ten minutes after the break the only miracle looked like Liverpool keeping the score down to three. Then, after 54 minutes, out of nothing Steven Gerrard headed in a Jon Arne Riise cross and the unthinkable happened – all in six bizarre and wonderful minutes. Smicer, then Alonso and it was all square. Six minutes!

Here's a few other things that take just six minutes:

- Grilling the perfect 1/4 inch rib-eye steak
- Watching Ronnie O'Sullivan's record-breaking 147 break at the 2001 World Championships
- Taking the Merseyrail from Liverpool James Street to Liverpool Central
- 1800 babies born globally
- 'Hotel California' by The Eagles

— MORE THAN COINCIDENCE —

While making their way to Istanbul in May 2005, many of the thousands of fans were talking omens. There were too many coincidences that year for Liverpool to fail. Here they are:

- In 1978 the Catholic Church mourned the death of Pope John Paul and Liverpool won their second European Cup. In 2005, Pope John Paul II died.
- In 1978, Wales won the Grand Slam. As they did in 2005.
- In 1981, when Liverpool won their third European cup, Britain was transfixed by two weddings. Prince Charles married Lady Diana and, perhaps more importantly, Ken Barlow married Deirdre in Coronation Street. In 2005, Charles was once more married, this time to Camilla Parker Bowles and Ken once more married Deidre.

— ANFIELD'S BALL PLAYING REVEREND —

James 'The Parson' Jackson was so much more than merely the captain of Liverpool Football Club (a position he held between 1929 and 1930).

Jackson, born in Newcastle to Scottish parents, was signed from Aberdeen in 1925 but had to wait a couple of years before becoming a regular in the team in a variety of positons, including centre half and inside right. What money he earned from playing for Liverpool he invested in his education, doing courses in philosophy and Greek, while also serving as an elder at a local church.

After he retired in 1933, Jackson went to Cambridge University and was then ordained as a reverend of the Presbyterian Church. As the Reverend Jackson, he officiated at the funeral in 1947 of the Liverpool chairman W.H. McConnell.

— SECONDS OUT, ROUND ONE! —

As well as tennis (see, *Anyone for Tennis*, page 68), boxing was another sport to regularly feature at Anfield throughout the 1920s and 1930s.

The most famous bout at the ground was fought by local fighter Ned Tarleton, who had impressed in the early part of the 1930s and earned himself a World Featherweight title shot against American Freddie Miller. On June 12th 1934, Tarleton fought Miller and although he gave a good account of himself, it was the American who retained the belt with a points decision. However, Tarleton did go on to become Commonwealth champion some six years later.

— LIVERPOOL'S FIRST CAPS —

- The first ever Liverpool player to win an England cap was Henry Bradshaw who in 1897 played for his country against Ireland at Trent Bridge in Nottingham. Despite the 6–0 victory, Bradshaw never won another cap.
- The first Liverpool player to win a Scotland cap was George Allan who in 1897 played in his country's 2–1 win over England at Crystal Palace.
- The first Liverpool player to win a cap for Wales was Maurice Parry, who on March 23rd 1901 played for his country against Ireland.
- The first Liverpool player to play for Northern Ireland was Bill Lacey, who in 1913 won his 11th cap against Wales.

— ALDO'S HOT STREAK —

On the last day of the 1986/87 season, John Aldridge scored in a 3–3 draw at Stamford Bridge. That game was Ian Rush's last for Liverpool before his move to Juventus, but the blow was softened by Aldridge's presence who went on to score in each of the first nine league games the following season. Aldridge's run of scoring in ten consecutive games was an English record before it was equalled by West Ham's Jermaine Defoe in 2000/01 while out on loan at Bournemouth.

Here are Aldridge's 1987 goals:

Date	Opposition	Venue	Goals	Score
May 9th	Chelsea	Stamford Bridge	1	3–3
Aug 15th	Arsenal	Highbury	1	2–1
Aug 29th	Coventry	Highfield Road	1 (pen)	4–1
Sep 5th	West Ham	Upton Park	1 (pen)	1–1
Sep 12th	Oxford	Anfield	1	2–0
Sep 15th	Charlton	Anfield	1 (pen)	3–2
Sep 20th	Newcastle	St James' Park	1	4–1
Sep 29th	Derby	Anfield	3 (1 pen)	4–0
Oct 3rd	Portsmouth	Anfield	1 (pen)	4–0
Oct 17th	Q.P.R	Anfield	1 (pen)	4–0

— MILESTONE LEAGUE GOALS —

It was Bill Shankly who called the league, Liverpool's "bread and butter", so here are the milestone goals in the club's first 114 years of League football:

Goal	Scorer	Date	Opposition
1	Malcolm McVean	Sep 2nd 1893	Middlesbrough Ironopolis
100	Thomas Bradshaw	Dec 8th 1894	Sheffield United
1000	Jack Parkinson	April 12th 1909	Sunderland
5000	Kenny Dalglish	March 25th 1979	Wolverhampton
6000	Jan Molby	March 23rd 1991	Derby County
7000	Andriy Voronin	Aug 25th 2007	Sunderland

At the end of the 2008/09 season Liverpool had scored 7,168 goals.

— A RED WINS GOLD —

Three Liverpool players have won Olympic Gold. In 1908, Arthur Berry, a barrister and the son of the Liverpool chairman who played four games for the club in two spells, was part of the British side that won the football tournament in London. Berry then went on to retain his gold medal in 1912 in Stockholm.

A team-mate of Berry's in 1912 was Joseph Dines who was part of the side that beat Denmark in the final. Dines signed for Liverpool shortly afterwards but played just once in a 2–1 win at Chelsea on September 9th 1912. He died on the Western Front in 1918.

Javier Mascherano matched Dines' feat in 2004, winning the Gold medal in the Athens Olympics with Argentina before joining Liverpool in 2007.

— SUPER CLUB, SUPER CUP —

Liverpool have contested the European Super Cup on five occasions. Originally, the match was between the European Cup and Cup Winners Cup winners, although now it is played between the winners of the Champions League and the UEFA Cup. The Reds' first Super Cup appearance was in 1977 when they played Hamburg (including recent Anfield departee Kevin Keegan) and won 7–1 on aggregate. Here is a full list of the games:

Date	Opposition	Score
Nov 22nd 1977	Hamburg (1st leg, A)	1–1
Dec 6th 1977	Hamburg (2nd leg, H)	6–0 (agg 7–1)
Dec 4th 1978	Anderlecht (1st leg, A)	1–3
Dec 19th 1978	Anderlecht (2nd leg, H)	2–1 (agg 3–4)
Jan 16th 1985	Juventus (A)	0–2*
Aug 24th 2001	Bayern Munich (Monaco)	3–2
Aug 26th 2005	CSKA Moscow (Monaco)	3–1 (aet)

* Liverpool could not find a free date to play the second leg. Fixture congestion also prevented the club from competing against Dinamo Tbilisi in 1981.

— TALLEST AND SMALLEST REDS —

Peter Crouch is Liverpool's tallest ever player

While 6ft 7in Peter Crouch is easily the tallest man ever to play for Liverpool, the smallest is a little less clear cut. Three players coming in at 5ft 4in have pulled on the red shirt of Liverpool: Robert Neil, James McBride and Mervyn Jones.

Neil was a Scot who played 27 games for the club between 1895 and 1897 (incredibly many of them were at centre-half!). Another Scot, McBride played from 1892 to 1895 and made 59 appearances. Finally, Jones, a Welsh outside-left played five times between 1952 and 1953.

— COMING TO A SCREEN NEAR YOU —

On March 11th 1967, Liverpool went to Goodison Park to play Everton in the fifth round of the FA Cup. 64,851 fans crammed into he stadium and such was the desire to see the first FA Cup Merseyside derby for 12 years, that giant close circuit television screens were put up at Anfield and attracted a further 40,109 fans. A total then of 104,960 fans saw Everton win 1–0.

— UNIVERSITY CHALLENGE —

Liverpool have long boasted university graduates in their team. Here are their details:

Player	Seasons	Degree	University
Gerald Powys Dewhurst	1893–94	N/A	Cambridge
Arthur Berry	1908–1912	N/A	Oxford
James Jackson	1925–1933	Philosophy and Greek	Liverpool
Brian Hall	1969–1976	Mathematics	Liverpool
Steve Heighway	1970–1981	Economics	Warwick
Mike Hooper	1986–1993	English Literature	Swansea

— THE END OF AN ERA —

On the face of it, Liverpool's 1–0 defeat at Watford in the sixth round of the FA Cup on February 21st 1970 was merely a humiliating exit at the hands of lower league opposition, but in fact it was much more important than that. The defeat at Vicarage Road was to be the alarm bell that woke Bill Shankly up to the fact that he had to change his team, the team that had put Liverpool so gloriously on the football map throughout the 1960s.

As the manager walked into the dressing-room it was with a heavy heart that he declared, "That's it, a lot of you have played your last game for Liverpool."

Shankly had been bringing in young players for while. The likes of Emlyn Hughes had played against Watford but players such as Steve Heighway, Brian Hall, Larry Lloyd and Ray Clemence were still learning and waiting in the reserves. The latter was brought straight in for the next league game, coming in for Tommy Lawrence in goal, a position Clemence would hold for eleven years. Roger Hunt had been sold before the cup defeat but would soon be followed out of Anfield by Ian St John, Ron Yeats and Peter Thompson as a new young breed of player came in who would soon bring another glut of trophies to the Liverpool public.

— IT'S A FAMILY AFFAIR —

On March 25th 1984, a corner of North London was turned into Merseyside for the day. For the first time Wembley was the venue for an all-Scouse showpiece when Liverpool faced Everton in the final of the League Cup (then the Milk Cup).

Liverpool, in their fourth successive final of the competition and about to claim their third successive championship were no strangers to the Twin Towers, but for Everton this was their first trip to the old place in seven years. The Blues, though, were about to embark on their most successful period that would see them win FA Cups, League Championships and European honours.

The game itself – a cautious 0–0 draw – was outshone by a fantastic atmosphere that saw blue and red mingling all over the ground. At the end of the game, with chants of 'Merseyside' ringing around the stadium, Liverpool and Everton players came together for an impromptu team group photo shoot. For the record (and city bragging rights), Liverpool won the replay 1–0 at Maine Road.

— RUSHIE, THE NIGHTMARE ON GLADYS STREET —

It was supposed to be Ian Rush's last Merseyside derby, so when he scored two goals against Everton at Anfield on April 25th 1987 to equal Dixie Dean's record of 19 derby goals, the place erupted. While the Kop sang his name, Evertonians wouldn't have been excused their own, albeit smaller party. After all, Rush, the man who couldn't stop scoring goals against them, was off, leaving the country, going to Italy, way out of harm's way.

That blue glee, however, would last just one season. In the summer of 1988, Rush came home. On May 20th 1989 the striker came on as a substitute at Wembley in the FA Cup final and in the fourth minute of extra-time scored to make the derby goals record his own. Oh, and he got another one that day to bring the cup back to Anfield. Rush finished his Liverpool career with 25 Merseyside derby goals, a record unlikely to be troubled in the near future.

— THE WELFARE STATE —

Local player Henry Welfare made his debut for Liverpool on February 15th 1913 in a league game at Anfield against Sheffield Wednesday. Two weeks later he scored his first goal against Derby but it was to be his only strike as he played just four games for the club.

At the end of the 1913/1914 season Welfare emigrated to Brazil, initially joining Corinthians before moving to Fluminense. Welfare, or 'Celso' as he was known in Brazil, was very popular and effective for the Rio club, helping them to win the State Championship three years in a row between 1917 and 1919. Welfare remained in Rio until his death in 1961.

— BACK AS A WINNING BOSS —

Having played in the red of Liverpool a selection of men have gone into management and come back to Anfield to win. That most famous of ex-Liverpool men, Matt Busby first did it on December 27th 1948, when his promising new Manchester United side came to Liverpool and won 2–0.

Here are three other managers who enjoyed returns to the Anfield dug-out:

Manager	Liverpool career	New Team	Date	Score
Jimmy Melia	1955–64	Brighton	Feb 20th 1983	1–2
Gordon Milne	1960–67	Leicester	Dec 26th 1984	1–2
Kenny Dalglish	1977–90	Blackburn	Sep 12th 1983	0–1

— RAY LAMBERT: A RED, MAN AND BOY —

Ray Lambert signed for Liverpool in 1936 at the tender age of 13, making him the youngest player to sign for the club. But the Welsh defender would have to wait a whole ten years before making his full debut for the Reds.

By the end of the Second World War, Lambert had got more than used to his surroundings and on January 5th 1946 he made his debut for the Reds at Chester in the third round (first leg) of the FA Cup. He wasn't alone. That afternoon eight players made their full debuts for the team, among them Bob Paisley, Bob Priday and Billy Liddell (who scored in a 2–0 win).

As for Lambert he went on to make 341 appearances for the Reds, scoring twice and winning a championship medal in 1947.

— LEND US A TENNER, ROBBIE LAD —

When *FourFourTwo magazine* published a football Rich List in 2008 the richest players in the country were revealed. Two former Reds made the top three, while current captain Steven Gerrard came in at number 10.

David Beckham led the way with a reported £112m fortune. Michael Owen was struggling in second place with just £37m and Robbie Fowler in third, thanks in part to a property portfolio which includes numerous properties in Merseyside, had amassed a comfortable £30m. By comparison, Gerrard was a relative pauper with assets worth £15m.

— RUSHIE AND THE MILK ADVERT —

In the late 1980s, an advert for milk featured two young Liverpudlian boys getting home from a game of football and arguing the merits of the drink.

Here's how the advert goes:

Boy 1: Got any lemonade?
Boy 2: If you want [takes out lemonade but serves himself milk.]
Boy 1: Milk? Uggghhh!
Boy 2: It's what Ian Rush drinks.
Boy 1: Ian Rush?
Boy 2: Yeah, and he said that if I didn't drink lots of milk, when I grow up I'd only be good enough to play for Accrington Stanley.
Boy 1: Accrington Stanley? Who are they?
Boy 2: Exactly!
[Boy 1 tries to grab the milk]
Boy 1: Gimmee some!
Boy 2: Nah, gerrof!
Boy 1: Gimmee some!

— WE SLAUGHTERED THEM —

Before putting on the number five jersey for Liverpool, big Ron Yeats worked as a slaughterman in an Aberdeen slaughterhouse.

— RED LEGENDS: JAMIE CARRAGHER —

"Number one is Carragher and number two is Carragher, number three is Carragher . . ." and so the chant goes on. "We all dream of a team of Carraghers, a team of Carraghers, a team of Carraghers." No player in the modern game has given more to the cause than Jamie Carragher, a player who no matter what the occasion, no matter whom the opposition, will give his all and for that unyielding grit and fight, the fans worship the very ground he walks on.

Their chant is not far off the truth. Carragher has played in nearly every position across the back four and the midfield and whilst he was good at full-back and in the holding midfield position it has been at centre-back that he has most excelled.

The decision to play him there was one of the first taken by Rafa Benitez when he arrived at Anfield in the summer of 2004. It was inspired. Carragher's partnership with Sami Hyypia at the heart of the defence drove Liverpool on in Europe. Their steely performances, most notably against Juventus and Chelsea took Liverpool to that incredible night in Istanbul where Carragher had perhaps his most famous game. He lunged, he tackled, he cleared, he barracked anyone he thought was giving up and at the end when it was all done, he made a beeline for the fans. All the acts of a legend.

Always accessible, always friendly, Carragher is a down-to-earth football man in an age when his kind are at a premium. Recently given a new and improved contract that will (hopefully) keep him at the club for the rest of career, no one can begrudge a man like Carragher being paid handsomely for a job he puts so much into and which he clearly adores.

Born in Bootle, Carragher came to Liverpool as a boy and was part of the Academy team that won the 1996 FA Youth Cup. Just months later he made his debut against Middlesbrough in the League Cup before scoring against Aston Villa at Anfield on his first Premiership start. Goals haven't flowed since but no matter, his place in Liverpool folklore is assured and fans can hope in their hearts that there is plenty more to come from a true hero.

Jamie Carragher fact-file

Appearances	577
Goals	5
England caps while at Liverpool	34

Honours	Season
FA Cup	2001
	2006

League Cup	2000/01
	2002/2003
Uefa Cup	2000/01
European Cup	2004/05
Charity Shield	2001
	2006

— THE FIRST TOSS OF A COIN —

Before Liverpool's first ever game at Anfield on September 3rd 1893, skipper Malcolm McVean called right and won the toss. Like so many of his successors, McVean chose to attack the Anfield Road end meaning Liverpool would be playing toward the Kop in the second period. Every Liverpool captain since has followed his example whenever they, too, have won the toss.

— SHANKS' LUNAR JIBE —

It may have been one giant leap for mankind, but it did little to impress Bill Shankly. After the first moon landing in July 1969, the Liverpool manager was asked to comment on what was the apparently monumental event.

"The moon? It's just like Goodison Park," he said. "There's no atmosphere."

— H'WAY THE LADS! —

A number of strikers from the north-east have scored goals for Liverpool. Here are the five most prolific:

Player	Seasons	Appearances	Goals
1. Harry Chambers	1919–1928	338	151
2. Albert Stubbins	1946–1953	178	83
3. Robbie Robinson	1904–1912	271	64
4. Peter Beardsley	1987–1991	175	59
5. David Hodgson	1982–1984	49	10

— CARSON'S UNDER-21 RECORD —

On June 17th 2007, Liverpool goalkeeper Scott Carson beat his club team-mate Jamie Carragher's record of 27 appearances (a record shared by Gareth Barry) for England's under-21s when he kept goal for the 28th time, against the Italians in the European under-21 Championships in Holland.

— TV REDS —

Liverpool Football Club, its players and fans have often appeared on the small screen in programmes which are not directly concerned with the action on the pitch. Here are a couple of the most memorable performances:

Boys from the Blackstuff, 1982

Alan Bleasdale's gritty drama centred on five unemployed tarmac layers from Liverpool. Each episode took a close look at one of the characters and in 'Yosser's Story', two of Liverpool's midfielders featured in a memorable scene. Yosser Hughes, played by Bernard Hill, takes his kids into a Liverpool bar, sees Graeme Souness sitting with Sammy Lee and sits in between the two of them staring intently at the then Liverpool captain, Souness.

Yosser:	You're Graeme Souness aren't you?
Souness:	Yeah.
Yosser:	You're famous . . .
Souness:	Well . . .
Yosser:	I'm Yosser Hughes.
Souness:	Pleased to meet you.
Yosser:	You look like me.
Souness:	Oh aye?
Yosser:	Magnum as well.
Souness:	Pardon?
Yosser:	Magnum, a detective. He used to be on television. An American.
Souness:	Oh aye. [Sammy Lee looks nervous]
Yosser:	[handing over a piece of paper] Sign this for us will ya, Graeme?
Souness:	Sure. Who's it for?
Yosser:	Me. Yosser Hughes. [Souness signs it]
Yosser:	[Reads it out loud] To Yosser Hughes. Better looking by far. Best wishes, Graeme Souness.

Scully, 1984

Originally a play by Alan Bleasdale, *Scully* was adapted for television in 1983 and featured a young Liverpudlian schoolboy who thought of nothing but Liverpool Football Club and what it would be like to one day play for them.

Francis Scully, played by Andrew Schofield, has fantasies about seeing

Kenny Dalglish, and the Liverpool legend appeared throughout the series in all sorts of scenes, from in his kit on the local park, to on the school stage dressed as a fairy-godmother. There is also a memorable scene in which Scully dreams that he is receiving the PFA Young Player of the Year award from Bob Paisley to applause from the Liverpool players, including Dalglish and Bruce Grobbelaar.

The opening credits to the series, which was originally broadcast on Channel 4 in six half-hour and one hour-long episode, include Scully running out at Anfield with the team and kicking a ball into the Kop. To make this look as real as possible the club allowed Schofield to run out with the side prior to a game against Everton at Anfield on March 19th 1983. The actor dressed in full kit and sporting the number 7 shirt runs to the Kop to be greeted (and this bit wasn't scripted) by chants of 'There's Only One Franny Scully.'

— AUNTIE BEEB'S GONG —

When Michael Owen won the Sports Personality of the Year award in 2001, he became the first and thus far only Liverpool player to win the award. On three occasions, however, Liverpool Football Club have been awarded the BBC's Team of the Year Award.

The first accolade came in 1977, after the European Cup triumph in Rome. The Reds then won it again in 1986 having won the Double and again in 2001 after the cup treble. If you are wondering why they didn't win it in 2005 after the miracle of Istanbul, England regained the Ashes that summer and got the vote.

— ONCE A BLUE, ALWAYS A BLUE? —

Not only did Wayne Rooney declare his lifelong allegiance to Everton before moving on to Manchester United, Goodison fans have had to put up with the nagging thought that some of Liverpool's best players started out as fans of the Toffees. Former Evertonians include:

Ian Rush
Steve McManaman
Robbie Fowler
Jamie Carragher
Michael Owen

— POOR SCOUSER TOMMY —

This chant dates back to the 1960s but was updated to include Ian Rush's four goals against Everton in 1982. The first part of the song comes from an American folk song called 'Red River Valley' that can be heard in John Huston's 1940 cinema classic *The Grapes of Wrath*. The second part of the song is from 'The Sash', a song sung by the Orange Order while the new addition at the end is from The Beatles hit, 'All You Need is Love'.

Let me tell you a story of a poor boy
Who was sent far away from his home
To fight for his king and his country
And also the old folks back home
So they put him in the Highland division
Sent him off to a far foreign land
Where the flies swarm around in their thousands
And there's nothing to see but the sand
Well the battle started next morning
Under the Arabian sun
I remember the poor Scouser Tommy
Who was shot by an old Nazi gun
As he lay on the battle field dying (dying dying)
With the blood rushing out of his head (of his head)
As he lay on the battle field dying (dying dying)
These were the last words he said . . .

Oh . . . I am a Liverpudlian
I come from the Spion Kop
I like to sing, I like to shout
I go there quite a lot (every week)
We are the team who plays in red
A team that we all know
A team that we call Liverpool
And to glory we will go
We've won the League
We've won the Cup
We've been to Europe too
We played the Toffees for a laugh
And we left them feeling blue

Five Nil!

One two
One two three

One two three four
Five nil !

Rush scored one
Rush scored two
Rush scored three
And Rush scored four!

La la la la la la la la!

All you need is Rush
All you need is Rush
All you need is Rush, Rush,
Rush is all you need

— FORTRESS ANFIELD —

On January 28th 1978, Birmingham City won 3–2 at Anfield in a First Division fixture that would turn out to be the Reds' last home defeat for nearly three years. The following fixture at Anfield was a 2–1 win over Arsenal in the League Cup, and this was followed by 84 more games in which visiting teams (in all competitions) failed to win at Liverpool's home ground. The run included the famous 7–0 win over Spurs in September 1978, three wins over Manchester United and a 10–1 win over Finnish side Oulun Palloseura in the European Cup in 1980.

"Before each game at Anfield we'd be sitting in the dressing-room," recalls Ray Kennedy. 'I'd be thinking, '1–0, 2–0? Yeah we'll win 2–0 today.' We just never thought we'd lose.'"

Eventually, of course, they did and it was bottom placed Leicester City, on 31st January 1981 who ended an historic sequence totalling 7,650 minutes of football. While Chelsea equalled Liverpool's run of 63 unbeaten league games at home at the end of the 2006/07 season, they have in that time lost twice in cup competitions.

— THE 51ST STATE —

The 51st State is a 2001 film set in Liverpool and starring Samuel L Jackson, Robert Carlyle and Ricky Tomlinson. The movie, a crime caper, sees Carlyle's character wearing a Liverpool shirt and the climax of the film is set at Anfield during a Liverpool-Manchester United game. During filming, Jackson is said to have become an ardent Liverpool fan.

143

— LIVERPOOL'S HALL OF FAME —

In 2002, Liverpool unveiled its Hall of Fame. Fans and ex-players were invited to send in nominations to a selection panel that consisted of Ian Callaghan, Alan Hansen, Phil Thompson, Brian Hall and Rick Parry which would choose two players from each decade to go in. The players who sit proudly in the Hall of Fame are:

Decade	Players
1892–1900	Harry Bradshaw, Matt McQueen
1900–1910	Alex Raisbeck, Jack Cox
1910–1920	Ephraim Longworth, Arthur Goddard
1920–1930	Elisha Scott, Donald McKinlay
1930–1940	Gordon Hodgson, Jimmy McDougall
1940–1950	Albert Stubbins, Jack Balmer
1950–1960	Billy Liddell, Alan A'Court
1960–1970	Ron Yeats, Roger Hunt
1970–1980	Ray Clemence, Ian Callaghan
1980–1990	Kenny Dalglish, Alan Hansen
1990–2000	John Barnes, Ian Rush

— THE (LONG) PATH TO GLORY —

In 1974, on the way to their second FA Cup victory, Bill Shankly's men had to play nine matches with three of the ties needing replays. Here's the run to cup glory:

Round	Opposition	Score
Third	Doncaster (H)	2–2
Third (replay)	Doncaster (A)	2–0
Fourth	Carlisle (H)	0–0
Fourth (replay)	Carlisle (A)	2–0
Fifth	Ipswich (H)	2–0
Quarter-final	Bristol City (A)	1–0
Semi-final	Leicester (Old Trafford)	0–0
Semi final (replay)	Leicester (Villa Park)	3–1
Final	Newcastle (Wembley)	3–0

— RED AND BLUE ARMBANDS —

The first skipper of Liverpool was Andrew Hannah who had been signed in 1892 from Renton FC. Hannah had also captained Everton prior to his new club being formed.

— THE JOINT PROGRAMME —

Despite the acrimonious split that led to the formation of a new football club in 1892, Everton and Liverpool did manage to share one thing in their early days – their programme. Each week for almost 50 years the programme would include the line-ups for a first team game, as well as those at the reserve games featuring both clubs. Liverpool's first programme cost 1p and went to great pains to explain the offside rule. In 1934, for the first time the two clubs began producing their own match-day reading.

— THE HALL OF FAME —

In 2002 the National Football Museum in Preston opened the English Football Hall of Fame to celebrate those who have best served the English game. To make the list, players or managers had to be 30-years-old or over and have played or managed in this country for at least five years. The inaugural list included two Liverpool players, Kevin Keegan and Kenny Dalglish, and two managers, Bill Shankly and Bob Paisley. Since then there have been a number of Liverpool men added to the list:

| 2005 | John Barnes |
| 2006 | Alan Hansen, Ian Rush, Roger Hunt |

— KEEPING IT IN THE FAMILY —

The following brothers, fathers and sons, and grandfathers and grandsons have played for Liverpool:

Brothers
Matt McQueen and Hugh McQueen
These brothers played together for Liverpool in the late 19th century. Matt, the eldest of the brothers, made his debut in 1892 and played 105 games before later becoming manager of the club. Hugh made his debut on the same day as Matt and went on to play 63 games.

Father and Son
Roy Saunders and Dean Saunders
Roy Saunders signed for Liverpool in May 1948 but had to wait until 1953 for his first team debut. He went on to make 146 appearances for the club. Saunders' son Dean came to Liverpool in 1991 for a then British record fee of £2.9m. He went on to make 61 appearances.

Grandfather and Grandson
Bill Jones and Rob Jones
Like so many, Bill's career was severely hampered by the Second World War. He signed in 1938 but didn't make his debut until 1946. Bill, a versatile performer, made 277 appearances for the club including the Reds' first ever game at Wembley in the 1950 FA Cup final. His grandson Rob arrived at the club in 1991 and made an immediate impression at right back going on to pay 243 games before injury cut short his career in 1999 aged just 27.

— RONNIE'S YEARS OF SERVICE —

Despite never being given the manager's job at Anfield, Ronnie Moran was a huge influence behind the scenes at Liverpool.

He joined the club in 1952 and was one of the shining lights in the troubled era that was the 1950s. A strong left back, his energy and enthusiasm would see him remain part of Bill Shankly's plans when he arrived and even won him a Championship medal as part of the 1963/64 winning team. Shankly obviously valued those attributes and asked Moran to join the backroom team when he retired in 1965. The most vocal member of Liverpool's dug-out, Moran would motivate and scold in equal measure, keeping the players' egos in check as the medals started to flood in. Former players tell of how Moran would walk around the dressing-room in pre-season handing out the last campaign's gongs from an old shoebox. "These count for nothing now, boys," he'd say. "Put them away and let's get on with this season."

Moran filled in as caretaker manager on two occasions, first when Kenny Dalglish resigned in 1991 and then a year later when Graeme Souness underwent open heart surgery, a procedure that allowed Moran to lead the team out at Wembley before the 1992 FA Cup final against Sunderland. Moran stayed at the club until 1998 after 46 years service to the Liverpool cause. To this day he remains a fan and is a regular visitor to Anfield. Listen carefully, you may hear him shouting.

— DOUBLE DEGEN —

Signed in the summer of 2008, Swiss international right-back Phillipp Degen has a twin brother David, who plays his football for FC Basle.

Selected bibliography

This book relied on a number of sources but the author would like to give a special mention of thanks to the following material:

Liverpool: A Complete Record 1892-1988
Brian Pead
Breedon Books 1988

The Anfield Encyclopedia: An A-Z of Liverpool FC
Stephen F. Kelly
Mainstream 1993

The Official Liverpool FC Illustrated History
Jeff Anderson with Stephen Done
Carlton 2002

www.liverpoolfc.tv

www.liverweb.com

www.lfchistory.net

— LIVERPOOL'S LEAGUE RECORD 1892–2007 —

Season	Div	P	W	D	L	F	A	W	D	L	F	A	Pts	Pos
1892/93	Lancs	22	10	0	1	44	7	7	2	2	22	12	36	1st
1893/94	2	28	14	0	0	46	6	8	6	0	31	12	50	1st (PR)
1894/95	1	30	6	4	5	38	28	1	4	10	13	42	22	16th (R)
1895/96	2	30	14	1	0	65	11	8	1	6	41	21	46	1st (PR)
1896/97	1	30	7	6	2	25	10	5	3	7	21	28	33	5th
1897/98	1	30	7	4	4	27	16	4	2	9	21	29	28	9th
1898/99	1	34	12	3	2	29	10	7	2	8	23	43	43	2nd
1899/00	1	34	9	4	4	31	19	5	1	11	18	26	33	10th
1900/01	1	34	12	2	3	36	13	7	5	5	23	22	45	1st(CH)
1901/02	1	34	8	3	6	28	16	2	9	6	14	22	32	11th
1902/03	1	34	11	3	3	48	21	6	1	10	20	29	38	5th
1903/04	1	34	7	5	5	24	20	2	3	12	25	42	26	17th (R)
1904/05	2	34	14	3	0	60	12	13	1	3	33	13	58	1st (PR)
1905/06	1	38	14	3	2	49	15	9	2	8	30	31	51	1st(CH)
1906/07	1	38	9	2	8	45	32	4	5	10	19	33	33	15th
1907/08	1	38	11	2	6	43	24	5	4	10	25	37	38	8th
1908/09	1	38	9	5	5	36	25	6	1	12	21	40	36	16th
1909/10	1	38	13	3	3	47	23	8	3	8	31	34	48	2nd
1910/11	1	38	11	3	5	38	19	4	4	11	15	34	37	13th
1911/12	1	38	8	4	7	27	23	4	6	9	22	32	34	17th
1912/13	1	38	12	2	5	40	24	4	3	12	21	47	37	12th
1913/14	1	38	8	4	7	27	25	6	3	10	19	37	35	16th
1914/15	1	38	11	5	3	45	34	3	4	12	20	41	37	14th

FIRST WORLD WAR

Season	Div	P	W	D	L	F	A	W	D	L	F	A	Pts	Pos
1919/20	1	42	12	5	4	35	18	7	5	9	24	26	48	4
1920/21	1	42	11	7	3	41	17	7	8	6	22	18	51	4th
1921/22	1	42	15	4	2	43	15	7	9	5	20	21	57	1st(CH)
1922/23	1	42	17	3	1	50	13	9	5	7	20	18	60	1st(CH)
1923/24	1	42	11	5	5	35	20	4	6	11	14	28	41	12th
1924/25	1	42	13	5	3	43	20	7	5	9	20	35	50	4th
1925/26	1	42	9	8	4	43	27	5	8	8	27	36	44	7th
1926/27	1	42	13	4	4	47	27	5	3	13	22	34	43	9th
1927/28	1	42	10	6	5	54	36	3	7	11	30	51	39	16th
1928/29	1	42	11	4	6	53	28	6	8	7	37	36	46	5th
1929/30	1	42	11	5	5	33	29	5	4	12	30	50	41	12th
1930/31	1	42	11	6	4	48	28	4	6	11	38	57	42	9th
1931/32	1	42	13	4	4	56	38	6	2	13	25	55	44	10th
1932/33	1	42	10	6	5	53	33	4	5	12	26	51	39	14th

Season	Div	P	W	D	L	F	A	W	D	L	F	A	Pts	Pos
1933/34	1	42	10	6	5	52	37	4	4	13	27	50	38	18th
1934/35	1	42	13	4	4	53	29	6	3	12	32	59	45	7th
1935/36	1	42	11	4	6	43	23	2	8	11	17	41	38	19th
1936/37	1	42	9	8	4	38	26	3	3	15	24	58	33	18th
1937/38	1	42	9	5	7	40	30	6	6	9	25	41	41	11th
1938/39	1	42	12	6	3	40	24	2	8	11	22	39	42	11th
SECOND WORLD WAR														
1946/47	1	42	13	3	5	42	24	12	4	5	42	28	57	1st(CH)
1947/48	1	42	9	8	4	39	23	7	2	12	26	38	42	11th
1948/49	1	42	5	10	6	25	18	8	4	9	28	25	40	12th
1949/50	1	42	10	7	4	37	23	7	7	7	27	31	48	8th
1950/51	1	42	11	5	5	28	25	5	6	10	25	34	43	9th
1951/52	1	42	6	11	4	31	25	6	8	7	26	36	43	11th
1952/53	1	42	10	6	5	36	28	4	2	15	25	54	36	17th
1953/54	1	42	7	8	6	49	38	2	2	17	19	59	28	22nd(R)
1954/55	2	42	11	7	3	55	37	5	3	13	37	59	42	11th
1955/56	2	42	14	3	4	52	25	7	3	11	33	38	48	3rd
1956/57	2	42	16	1	4	53	26	5	10	6	29	28	53	3rd
1957/58	2	42	17	3	1	50	13	5	7	9	29	41	54	4th
1958/59	2	42	15	3	3	57	25	9	2	10	30	37	53	4th
1959/60	2	42	15	3	3	59	28	5	7	9	31	38	40	3rd
1960/61	2	42	14	5	2	49	21	7	5	9	38	37	52	3rd
1961/62	2	42	18	3	0	68	19	9	5	7	31	24	62	1st (PR)
1962/63	1	42	13	3	5	45	22	4	7	10	26	37	44	8th
1963/64	1	42	16	0	5	60	18	10	5	6	32	27	57	1st(CH)
1964/65	1	42	12	5	4	42	33	5	5	11	25	40	44	7th
1965/66	1	42	17	2	2	52	15	9	7	5	27	19	61	1st(CH)
1966/67	1	42	12	7	2	36	17	7	6	8	28	30	51	5th
1967/68	1	42	17	2	2	51	17	5	9	7	20	23	55	3rd
1968/69	1	42	16	4	1	36	10	9	7	5	27	14	61	2nd
1969/70	1	42	10	7	4	34	20	10	4	7	31	22	51	5th
1970/71	1	42	11	10	0	30	10	6	7	8	12	14	51	5th
1971/72	1	42	17	3	1	48	16	7	6	8	16	14	57	2nd
1972/73	1	42	17	3	1	45	19	8	7	6	27	23	60	1st(CH)
1973/74	1	42	18	2	1	34	11	4	11	6	18	20	57	2nd
1974/75	1	42	14	5	2	44	17	6	6	9	16	22	51	2nd
1975/76	1	42	14	5	2	41	21	9	9	3	25	10	60	1st(CH)
1976/77	1	42	18	3	0	47	11	5	8	8	15	22	57	1st(CH)
1977/78	1	42	15	4	2	37	11	9	5	7	28	23	57	2nd
1978/79	1	42	19	2	0	51	4	11	6	4	34	12	68	1st(CH)

Season	Div	P	W	D	L	F	A	W	D	L	F	A	Pts	Pos
1979/80	1	42	15	6	0	46	8	10	4	7	35	22	60	1st(CH)
1980/81	1	42	13	5	3	38	15	4	12	5	24	27	51	5th
1981/82*	1	42	14	3	4	39	14	12	6	3	41	18	87	1st(CH)
1982/83	1	42	16	4	1	55	16	8	6	7	32	21	82	1st(CH)
1983/84	1	42	14	5	2	50	12	8	9	4	23	20	80	1st(CH)
1984/85	1	42	12	4	5	36	19	10	7	4	32	16	77	2nd
1985/86	1	42	16	4	1	58	14	10	6	5	31	23	88	1st(CH)
1986/87	1	42	15	3	3	43	16	8	5	8	29	26	77	2nd
1987/88	1	40	15	5	0	49	9	11	7	2	38	15	90	1st(CH)
1988/89	1	38	11	5	3	33	11	11	5	3	32	17	76	2nd
1989/90	1	38	13	5	1	38	15	10	5	4	40	22	79	1st(CH)
1990/91	1	38	14	3	2	42	13	9	4	6	35	27	76	2nd
1991/92	1	42	13	5	3	34	17	3	11	7	13	23	64	6th
1992/93	Prem	42	13	4	4	41	18	3	7	11	21	37	59	6th
1993/94	Prem	42	12	4	5	33	23	5	5	11	26	32	60	8th
1994/95	Prem	42	13	5	3	38	13	8	6	7	27	24	74	4th
1995/96	Prem	38	14	4	1	46	13	7	7	6	24	21	71	3rd
1996/97	Prem	38	10	6	3	38	19	9	5	5	24	18	68	4th
1997/98	Prem	38	13	2	4	42	16	5	9	5	26	26	65	3rd
1998/99	Prem	38	10	5	4	44	24	5	4	10	24	25	54	7th
1999/00	Prem	38	11	4	4	28	13	8	6	5	23	17	67	4th
2000/01	Prem	38	13	4	2	40	14	7	5	7	31	25	69	3rd
2001/02	Prem	38	12	5	2	33	14	12	3	4	34	16	80	2nd
2002/03	Prem	38	9	8	2	30	16	9	2	8	31	25	64	5th
2003/04	Prem	38	10	4	5	29	15	6	8	5	26	22	60	4th
2004/05	Prem	38	12	4	3	31	15	5	3	11	21	26	58	5th
2005/06	Prem	38	15	3	1	32	8	10	4	5	25	17	82	3rd
2006/07	Prem	38	14	4	1	39	7	6	4	9	18	20	68	3rd
2007/08	Prem	38	12	6	1	43	13	9	7	3	24	15	76	4th
2008/09	Prem	38	12	7	0	41	13	13	4	2	36	14	86	2nd

CH = Champions
PR = Promoted
R = Relegated

* Three points for a win introduced